Leif Eriksson published his debut novel in 1979 and has since written and ghostwritten a number of books.

Martin Svensson published his debut novel in 2007. Since then he has written twenty books.

Leif and Martin began writing together in 2010 and have since worked on several projects.

The Mauler

Alexander Gustafsson tells his story to
Leif Eriksson and Martin Svensson

HODDER &
STOUGHTON

First published in Great Britain in 2016 by
Hodder & Stoughton
An Hachette UK company

First published in paperback in 2017

A CIP catalogue record for this title is available from the British Library

ISBN 978 1 473 64802 9

Typeset in Adobe Garamond by Palimpsest Book Production Limited,
Falkirk, Stirlingshire

Printed and bound by Clays Ltd, St Ives plc

Hodder & Stoughton policy is to use papers that are natural, renewable and
recyclable products and made from wood grown in sustainable forests. The
logging and manufacturing processes are expected to conform to the
environmental regulations of the country of origin.

Hodder & Stoughton Ltd
Carmelite House
50 Victoria Embankment
London EC4Y 0DZ

www.hodder.co.uk

Contents

	Prologue	I
1.	Farmer Ove	7
2.	The Black Brothers	15
3.	Lads	31
4.	Fuck the World	41
5.	The West Coast Family	51
6.	Gladius	65
7.	The Road to UFC	77
8.	Pro and Poor	89
9.	Alliance	101
10.	Down Under	111
11.	The Mauler versus The Hammer	121
12.	New Year Fireworks in Vegas	129
13.	UFC Sweden	139
14.	Shogun	149
15.	Jon 'Bones' Jones	157
16.	MMA Explodes	169
17.	Waiting for the Rematch	177
18.	Bad Boys in Newcastle	183
19.	Injury	189
20.	Anthony 'Rumble' Johnson	197
21.	For the Win	205
	Acknowledgements	210
	Selected Titles and Awards	211
	Swedish MMA Rules	215
	Picture Credits	232

Prologue

Prologue

It was the biggest house I had ever seen, at least 5,000 square metres. An old hospital for kids and heart patients. Now it was a secure home for addicts and criminals. It was called the West Coast Family, and lay all by itself out in the countryside between Gothenburg and the town of Borås.

When I arrived that summer day I was nineteen and carrying a two-year sentence in an open prison. I didn't really know what to expect as I went up the steps with my bag slung over my shoulder. After saying hello to some of the staff I was shown into a room where I was told to sit down on a chair. A guy who had come in just after me was put on a chair next to me. He was older with long hair. He looked worn down.

'Niklas,' he said, stretching out his hand.

'Alex,' I replied as I took it. 'You know what is going on here?'

I glanced at the two members of staff who had shown us to the room. They were at a table with their backs turned to us, fiddling with something.

'OK, lads,' one of them said. He had introduced himself earlier as Danne.

In his hand was a pair of clippers with a long cord. He plugged them into a socket behind us, and before I had time to grasp what was happening he had started to take off all of my hair.

I already had fairly short hair, so I didn't care too much. But I did wonder how Niklas would take it when Danne turned to do him as well.

'Ready?'

Niklas seemed anything but ready. But what could he say? The clippers buzzed into life again and his long blond curls fell to the floor.

I gave Niklas a month max at that place. It turned out I was wrong. That junkie was much tougher than he looked with his sunken cheeks and sad eyes.

'Right,' said Danne and looked at us. 'Time to get you some rooms. But might you want something to eat first?'

We ate reheated lasagne in a huge and empty dining-hall. Then we were told to go to the reception. Danne gave us each bedclothes and a schedule.

I looked at my schedule as I followed him up a creaking staircase. It began with being woken up at four-thirty, followed by making the beds, cleaning the rooms, putting on gym kit, and doing a hundred press-ups and sit-ups. We then had to shift ourselves 10K. After 'running' came 'cooking duty'. I asked Danne's huge back what that meant.

He replied without turning around. 'We have a rolling schedule. You start by making breakfast, lunch and dinner. If you don't do it, you'll quickly become unpopular.'

Danne explained that if you broke the rules by sleeping in, missed attendance or deviated from the schedule in any other way, it was not just you who got punished but everyone. Later on I would see with my own eyes and experience first-hand exactly how tough the punishments could be.

We came to a corridor at the top of the stairs. Niklas was given a room and did not look terribly happy as he went in and closed the door behind himself.

When we were eating he had talked a lot about his kids and I thought how much he must have been missing them. I was given a room at the very end of the hallway and also felt very down once I was left alone inside it. Still, there was something about the place that I liked. I could not put my finger on what it was exactly, but for the first time in a long while it felt important to make an effort. It would be hard, I knew that. But nothing could be worse than what I had just gone through.

I made the bed and lay down on it fully clothed. I had only planned on resting a bit, but suddenly all the tension that had built up during the day was released. I was out like a light.

When I woke up again it was four. That meant half an hour until wake-up call. Going back to sleep was pointless.

I got out of bed and straightened the sheets. Then I put on my gym stuff and sat waiting on the edge of the bed with a nervous ache in my stomach.

At four-thirty on the dot someone began hammering on the doors in the corridor. When they reached mine I opened it and shouted, 'Up!' Not long after, all the guys were assembled in the hall on the ground floor.

One of the staff, who also had exercise kit on, greeted all the newcomers. 'Right, let's go!' he shouted.

We all started on our hundred press-ups and sit-ups.

I have always liked exercise, so the press-ups, sit-ups, and the 10K run through the woods in the light summer morning only served to get me going. Some of the others, on the other hand, gave out pretty quick. The military discipline was not to everyone's taste. The truth was that a lot of the guys I ran alongside that morning would crack completely later on.

When we arrived back, we had to go straight to the kitchen and get breakfast ready. At home Mum would have taken care of the food, so it felt strange, but most of all it was stressful. At half six we were called again for physical training, something we had to do each morning before being allowed to eat.

We stood in line with some of the staff across from us. I noticed how one of them was sort of eyeing me.

'New here, right?'

I nodded.

'You done much training before?'

'Yeah, boxing. When I was younger.'

'You can see that . . . I see it in your body language.'

The guy, at least twenty years older than me, was called Carlos. He explained that he had done a good bit of fighting himself and asked if we could maybe train together.

'Uh, yeah . . . 'course,' I said.

Carlos took me under his wing. We got a feel for each other in no time at all. In that first session we buzzed along like two old buddies. When the day was over I could not feel anything but grateful for ending up there, even if the journey had been long, and at times extremely painful.

Chapter 1
Farmer Ove

veryone in my family is religious. It isn't like we don't drink or swear, or that we go to church every Sunday, but we pray. For my part I truly believe that has helped me many times.

Dad was a lumberjack. Mum was a temp on farms milking cows. When they had me, they hired a house on a little farm between Sala and Västerås, north of Stockholm.

They argued the whole time. Often it was to do with Dad's drinking. He couldn't take responsibility. When they were going to get married, for example, it came out that he was already married to a woman in Spain. Even so, they managed to stay together on-and-off for another year until my little sister Elina was born.

Dad was unemployed by that point and was on the drink more than ever. Elina got seriously ill, too. It turned out she had swelling in her brain tissue and there was an abscess growing inside. One half of her brain was under pressure. I can't remember anything about what happened, of course, but Mum told me how they were rushed to the University Hospital in Uppsala by ambulance, where Elina had surgery. We were near to losing her. At one point her heart even stopped beating. Mum prayed for her, though. A priest came to the hospital and prayed for her as well. In the end things turned out alright, unlikely as it seemed.

During her recovery, one of the doctors said that Elina must have had a guardian angel – seven in ten kids who have the condition end up with serious brain damage.

Soon after Elina came out of hospital, Mum could no longer make it work with Dad. But she did not leave him. Instead she gave him an ultimatum. 'If you want a future with me and the kids, we can live apart for a bit. You can get yourself a job and what not, and then we can give it a go.'

She was giving him one final chance to set things right. Instead he borrowed 50,000 Swedish kronor from my uncle and they both vanished to Thailand. Mum was left alone, looking after two kids.

Mum said to me that Dad was the love of her life and that it was the worst thing to ever happen to her. That came from a woman who had been through a lot already. Moreover, she would have to cope with everything I brought upon us later.

But this was the summer of 1988 and I was only one year old, happily ignorant of everything to come.

For the few weeks that Mum and Elina had been at the hospital, my grandma had taken care of me. She lived in a little house on the family farm in a place called Godby. Because Mum was now on her own with the two of us kids, it was decided that we would all move in to the big house next door. It was my uncle's, but as he was in Thailand with Dad, the place was empty.

That autumn Mum got farm work in Västra Skedvi nearby and travelled between five different farms to milk. She got up at four or five in the morning, and when the coldest winter in many years arrived, it was not rare for it to be minus twenty outside.

Grandma helped as much as she could. She came in and gave me and Elina breakfast. She got us ready and drove us to the child-minder, a woman called Mona who lived in Arboga. Then she went off to her own job as a cook at the women's open prison in Frövi. It took her almost an hour to get there. When she was done at four, she drove all the way back to Arboga to collect me and Elina. Then she would make dinner for us back on the farm in Godby. Mum didn't get home until eight or nine at night.

For Grandma there was no question that she would take care of us. She was a refugee from the war in Finland and had been taken in by someone herself. Eventually me and Elina moved in with her. It was simpler. Grandma had no spare room, so we slept in her bed all together. She has told us time and again how wild we were. All she had to do was leave us for two minutes and there would be porridge on the floor, walls and ceiling.

Everyone in my family is religious. It isn't like we don't drink or swear, or that we go to church every Sunday, but we pray. For my part I truly believe that has helped me many times. As soon as me and Elina learned to speak we would shout for Mum to come and read us the Lord's Prayer at bedtime. That whole winter a priest would visit us to read from the Bible with Mum and Grandma. His name was Börje and he was a Baptist. Mum and Grandma used to pray with him for everything to be OK. That meant me, Elina and Mum's work, which was taking its toll on her.

Eventually Dad returned. He and Mum became friends once more and Mum wanted to try again. But they couldn't. The feeling of being let down had left its mark on her, and I think she'll carry it for the rest of her life. Me, Elina, Mum and Grandma carried on as before, until Mum met Kalle. The first farm on Mum's milking route was in Boda, where he lived. As time passed they became good friends, and everyone close to her thought they should get together. In May 1990 they got engaged, and three months later they were married at a big house called Jäderbruk.

Mum told me that in the middle of the vows, which were overseen by Börje the Baptist, I jumped straight up into the air. She and Kalle heard a thud and saw my legs sticking up from behind the altar. Presumably I must have been bored. I have always been restless and I could never sit still. When a doctor took a look at me later on he said I ticked four of the six boxes for an ADHD diagnosis. That was why life on the farm suited me so well. There was space to run about and always something to do. I rode around on the tractor with Kalle, climbed anything in sight, and thumped Elina or shot her with an air rifle loaded with unripened berries. Elina thought I was a complete idiot, but I didn't care. I had so much energy to get rid of, and usually it was offloaded onto her.

Family has always been important to me and I quickly started counting Kalle as one of our own. In 1991 he and Mum had a daughter, Erika. I would go on to have two more half-sisters, Elisabeth and Evelina. But it was always Elina I would home in on. She did not get a moment's peace from me. I always wanted to do something. I remember when I worked out that you could hang off Kalle's cuckoo clock on the kitchen wall. Kalle's dad had built it and it was screwed straight into the wall, so you could hang off it no problem. When I convinced Elina she should join me, however, the whole thing was ripped from the wall and crashed to the floor. As I heard Mum come running, I hissed at Elina, 'Hide under the table.' Then I ran off to a much better hiding place. In my family everyone has a bit of a temper, not least Mum. Because Elina was the first one to be found, she also took the brunt of it.

Even though we had moved over to Boda, me and Elina still stayed with Grandma in Godby some weeks. She was always an extra mother to us, but sometimes even she could lose patience. She used to have a bundle of birch twigs on the wall and would say, 'Any mischief and you'll feel the birch wood.' Unfortunately such threats had no impact on me, so once she actually came after me with it. That time *I* was the one who hid under the kitchen table. Elina saw me, pointed at me and said 'Alex' loudly. It was over.

Soon after Mum married Kalle, Dad moved up north to Skellefteå. Me and Elina didn't see him for several years. Mum talked about him a lot, though, as if she wanted to remind us we had a biological father. They'd had their issues, but she could not bring herself to judge the man. Her own dad, my grandfather, was also an alcoholic and had died at fifty-three. So she knew what it was like. One summer day, as I was about to start first grade, she said, 'I want you to meet your real dad.'

Elina and me sat at the table. Mum stood over the stove. She did it a lot at that time. Me and my sisters really did get the best food in the world: home-slaughtered meat, potatoes from the yard, and unpasteurised milk brought in by Mum in three-litre buckets from the barn. Grandma says that's why I ended up being so big and tall. I can't recall exactly how me and Elina reacted to the suggestion, but it must have sounded a fun proposition to our ears, because a few days later Mum presented us with plane tickets.

It must have been the first time me and Elina flew. It was the first time we had flown by ourselves in any case.

Mamma drove us to Arlanda airport in Stockholm, and before

we said goodbye she hung signs around our necks with our names on.

Both of us must have been excited about it all. From what I recall we didn't argue one bit, just walked quietly off to wait for the plane.

Dad, whose name to everyone else was Håkan Larsson, was tall and thin with a moustache. Apart from the dark hair we look quite similar. He used snuff, too, a brand of loose tobacco called Ettans. He stuffed it under his lip in the biggest clumps I have ever seen, half a tin at a time. Another thing about Dad was that he had a sense of humour, and when Mum occasionally spoke to him on the phone she could laugh so much her eyes watered. He was waiting for us by the baggage carousel at Skellefteå airport and waving. We hadn't seen each other in years, so it all felt a bit strange. We had photos of him at home, and had spoken on the phone and Mum helped us to write letters, but I had no memories from the time we lived together. Even so, it was still great to see him.

Dad lived in a rented apartment together with his mother, my other Grandma, and worked in the woods for a forestry company. I don't remember the layout of the apartment exactly, only that the furniture was very old-fashioned. But it was clean and bright and we had a good time, presumably because Dad was entirely sober those few days.

For as long as I can think of, I have loved competing and hated losing, and as a kid I was able to try all kinds of sports; football and hockey but others, too. However, I've never been a team player and never liked the idea that winning or losing should depend on anyone else. I have to admit that the fights and the adrenalin kicks are what attracted me. I have always liked wrestling and fighting. When I started at school in Medåkers that autumn, a few kilometres from Boda, I had my first contact with someone with similar inclinations. His name was Björn and like me he took the bus to school. Because Medåkers was just a village school, a lot of us rode in together. The first, second and third graders all shared one class. There were three separate classrooms for us and then another two for the fourth and fifth graders.

One day me and Björn started fighting. Maybe I grabbed hold of him, or perhaps he smacked me, but after that we took each other on every morning as we waited for the bus. We stopped as if nothing had happened as soon as the bus pulled up at the kerb. The other kids always knew what was coming and stood in a circle cheering us on.

In school itself things went fine enough. Well, fine is maybe an exaggeration. I have no patience for sitting still and reading, and I am not that practical either. I was also hopelessly insecure and shy. More than anything else I was shy around girls, something which is still kind of true now. Apart from the fights with Björn, I was almost invisible in infant and junior school. Nonetheless, I enjoyed being there in the company of the teachers and my classmates.

It got worse when I moved on to sixth grade at the Stureskolan school in Arboga, the bigger town nearby. First of all I was a bit chunky, and on top of that I came from the country and was dressed differently to everyone else. I did what I could to blend in, getting some new clothes and learning some new words, but it was hard. However you looked at it, I was a farm boy, and even though I wouldn't say Arboga was a metropolis today, back then it was the big city.

On the farm in Boda we had a bull who weighed over a ton, called Ove. He was so heavy that he broke the cows' backs when he tried to mate with them. Someone found out about this, and soon everyone started calling me Farmer Ove. It was a name that would follow me for some time to come.

Chapter 2
The Black Brothers

I was totally naked. There was no furniture. If I needed to go for a piss there was a drain in the floor.

The first guy I ever really properly fought with was Camilo, who came from El Salvador. It was in the sports hall. I can't remember what kicked everything off, but I guess that like a lot of other people, he had taunted me about something. Me and Camilo went at each other pretty thoroughly, in any case, and we were both given detention. Before we could leave the classroom our teacher made us shake hands. As amazing as it sounds, on the way home we became mates.

Through Camilo I soon got to know Wilson, Fernando and Jimmy. Camilo and Jimmy were childhood friends who hung around with each other the whole time. Jimmy was a year older and already in seventh grade. We had met earlier a few times, but now we were friends for real. We were made of the same stuff. We both had the same energy and got bored if nothing happened. Jimmy's background was a bit different to mine, though. Both his mum and dad had alcohol problems and he had ended up living with different foster families. He never moaned about it, but I got the sense that he'd had it tough.

Soon enough I lost contact with my old friends from the village, but made new ones by defending myself with my fists. I was tall and strong, and I liked the confidence and approval that came with being good at fighting. It was a world where I could stand on my own two feet. I became someone, for better or worse. Everyone but Jimmy was an immigrant: Mexicans, Chileans and other Latino guys. I got to know several of them in the same way I had first met Camilo, after going at them a few rounds.

Later that autumn Jimmy managed to get hold of two beat-up cars and somehow get them out to the farm in Boda. We drove around like maniacs and smashed into each other. We called ourselves the Dalton Brothers, wrote the letters DB on the cars and listened to sixties rock. When I turned thirteen, we each bought ourselves a moped and burned about on them. Jimmy had a Puch Dakota and I had a Montana. About the same time, it must have been Jimmy's birthday or something, he arranged a party at his dad's place.

It was the first time I ever drank, and because I don't do things by halves, I chugged down a whole crate of light beer and got so drunk that I pissed all over my trousers when I tried to go behind a bush. Jimmy rang Grandma and told her what had happened. It was always Grandma we turned to when we had problems. She came straight away. The day after, she and Mum both let me have it, but it made little difference. The next weekend they ordered me to stay at home, so I took the moped into town. The weekend after that, when they confiscated the moped, the guys came by and gave me a lift.

We were wild even in school. Once me, Jimmy and Wilson raced to see who could get to the lunch-hall first. I don't recall who won, but when we got there we held the doors so nobody else could get in. A girl stuck her arm through the gap without us seeing and we ended up breaking it by accident. She let out a piercing scream and we all got shit scared.

We ran up to the top floor and waited for class to start again. Instead we were asked to visit the head teacher. It had been a genuine accident and we were all really sorry it had happened. Afterwards we went to find the girl and gave her flowers and chocolates to apologise. She looked quite shaken when she laid eyes on us, so we told her not to be scared and wrote on her plaster cast. I have no idea if it made her any less scared, but it felt good to be able to say sorry for what had happened.

As I said, I was always restless and had trouble sitting still, but until then I had at least been able to sit in the classroom and take part. Now I began to skip off. So did my new friends, Camilo, Wilson and Jimmy. Soon enough we found ourselves in a special needs class of our own, which changed nothing. Nobody at that school liked us. Not the teachers, and not the students. But there was one teacher who was different – my tutor, Gert. We thought he might be gay, but he was a sound guy. He seemed to get us and did as much as he could. Another thing that set Gert apart was that he owned an old Rolls-Royce, and one day he asked if we wanted to go and see it. It was a stupid question.

'Going well,' said one of us.

'I worked hard for this,' replied Gert.

He tried to get us to understand that it could pay to work hard and get an education. We knew he wanted the best for us. That was why we jumped to his defence a little while later when he became the victim. In our special needs class there was a girl who got angry during a lesson and screamed 'fucking queer!' at him. Gert was always super cool, but he flipped. Before anyone had time to react, he had picked up a desk and thrown it at her. The girl burst into tears and ran out the room.

Gert put the desk back in its place and looked at us. We looked back. It was completely silent. Then the head and the school counsellor walked in. The head said the girl had accused Gert of throwing a desk. We all shouted, 'She's lying! She's lying! She lies all the time!' at once. We reckoned she had been out of order and didn't deserve any sympathy. Soon after that the girl was suspended. We never discussed it with Gert, but he was our friend for the whole of our time at Stureskolan.

In Arboga at the beginning of the 2000s there were a whole load of different groups: the classic car guys, the far-right gangs, and the Mexican and Latino immigrants that me and Jimmy hung about with. We felt like they accepted us. If something happened, then we had each other's backs. The far-right guys would call us names like 'The Black Brothers', both at school and in town. The first run-in that I had with the police for assault was the result of one such encounter. It was during gym class at the end of seventh grade. The guy, who was in the same class, shouted 'Traitor' or something similar and just went for me. I was better at fighting, though. This meant he was bleeding more than me when it was all over, and I was the one who got in trouble for it.

My sister Elina, a year younger, had also started at Stureskolan by then. Almost immediately she was drawn into all our shit, and without asking for it she was soon an integral part of what we did. We used to swing open the door to her classroom and shout for her to join us. Nobody save her classmates knew what her name was. Everyone just called her Ove's sis. It was her identity from the start of seventh grade. She worked hard and wasn't part of all the mischief we got up to, but she was guilty by association. For example, one time we got a fire extinguisher and sprayed it all over a corridor. She got three days of detention. It must have been hell for Mum back then. Quite how bad it was I wouldn't realise until much later.

That summer me and my mates partied a lot. I had been given my own little cabin on the farm we could hang in. If we were out in Arboga we would break into Gomez's place. He was a thirty-five-year-old handicapped guy from South America with learning difficulties. There would be sixteen or seventeen of us and we would just take over his apartment on Friday and Saturday nights. One of us would climb in through the window and open the door for the other. When Gomez came home later in the evening it was like a battle royal in there. It wasn't right. We exploited and abused him completely. At the weekends we would fight with each other for a laugh. We pitched Swedes against immigrants, but Jimmy and me were the only Swedes, so we had a hard time of it when we tried to give each other wedgies and mess about. Once me and Jimmy started playfighting and I landed on his foot so it gave out. At first I didn't notice, I only heard his scream. I looked at him as he sat on the floor.

'Don't you touch my foot,' he whined.

'And if I do?' I asked.

'I promise you I will go mental.'

I looked at the foot. It had already begun to swell up, and before Jimmy could react I picked it up and bent it in the other direction. He flew up from where he was sitting and hit me as hard as he could in the back. It fucking hurt, and we resented each other for a while after that, even if we did eventually get over it.

Another activity we devoted ourselves to around then was car theft. Ford Escorts were the easiest. I would smash the windscreen while someone else jumped in and snapped the steering lock with their foot. Then you opened the dashboard with a screwdriver and out came a bit of plastic that looked like a lump of sugar. If you stuck the screwdriver in and turned it, then nine times out of ten the thing would start. We would just drive around and crash them. We would often drink at the same time, so it was always kind of crazy. I'm not sure we even once considered we might get arrested for it. When we headed back to my cabin we would simply abandon the car in a ditch a few hundred metres away.

Thankfully Mum never found out about everything I was doing, but she knew about a lot of it. One day when I came into the house to eat breakfast she had had enough. 'I think you need to move up and live with your dad for a while,' she said. I guess she thought it would be good to get me out of Arboga and away from the guys I was hanging around with.

Mum helped me pack and drove me and my stuff all the way up to Dad's place. I started at a school in town in Skellefteå. I had only been there a few days when I ended up in a fight again. Soon the school got in touch with Mum, who had to buy me a plane ticket so I could go home again. Elina had also been up north visiting and the plan was for us to go home together. Dad would drive us to the airport. The problem was that he was drinking too much around then, and a few hours before we were supposed to leave, he got up and said he was 'just popping over to see the neighbours'.

Me and Elina sat and waited in the kitchen. Suddenly we both sensed he had been gone too long, and because we had a flight to catch we both got more and more stressed.

'When do you think he'll come back?' asked Elina.

I got up, went to the phone and rang Mum.

'What's wrong?' was the first thing she said.

I explained that Dad had gone to see a neighbour and not come back. Mum said we should get our things and wait outside. We did as we were told and she rang a taxi for us.

I was never angry with Dad for his drinking or his absence when I was growing up. I see alcoholism as a disease and know he didn't have the resources to take care of a whole family. I do miss him, though, especially now.

The idea was I would only be home a few days, enough time for Mum to sit down and have a chat with me. When it was time to go back she dropped me back at Arlanda airport, but I couldn't bring myself to get on the flight. I guess it was a panic attack, because suddenly I started shaking. Eventually I had to ring Mum.

'I can't do it,' I told her. 'I can't go back.'

Mum could hear in my voice that I was deadly serious, because she told me to take a train to Västerås and she would collect me from there. I never went back to Skellefteå, but I kept in touch with Dad over the phone. Sometimes I wrote him letters too.

As I said, I had no shortage of different sports to try out, but it was when I was fourteen and started to box at the BK Köping club that I found something that really worked for me. Mum and Grandma both threw themselves behind me. They got me into the club, and Mum would drive me to and from training. Grandma even cleaned the gym. I guess they thought it was positive I had finally found something to occupy me, and you could see I had a talent for it.

Unfortunately there weren't that many fixtures to fight and after a while I started to get tired of it. I'm the kind of guy who has to compete. If I can't do that, there is no point to it. I fought about ten fights and won all of them. I stopped with the boxing when I was sixteen, but still managed to become Swedish junior heavyweight champion.

Apart from Jimmy, Wilson and Camilo, I also used to hang around with a guy called Alvaro from Mexico and another called Domiku from Chile. Like me, Domiku was shy around girls. When we hung out together we used to chat and joke around, but as soon as a girl came near he would go completely silent. Back then he had a shaved head, a fat gold chain around his neck and a big signet ring, and I think he also used to wear a T-shirt with the Chilean flag on it. Domiku was an easygoing and caring guy, but tread on his toes and he flipped.

Another one of the gang was Antonio. It was him who first called me Farmer Ove. He was much older, which meant we looked up to him. One day in the summer holidays between eighth and ninth grade we were over at Domiku's house playing on the console. I always got restless sitting in front of the TV for hours, and Jimmy wasn't a fan of computer games at all. He did love hot dogs, though, so after a few hours at Domiku's he started making noises about going to buy some.

'Please, let's go get some,' he said.

I started to get tired of Jimmy's moaning, so me and Wilson went out with him. Domiku lived in a block of rental flats on the edge of Arboga, and a short walk away was a petrol station called Bilisten where they sold hot dogs. It was the middle of the day and quite hot, but even so Jimmy had a blue denim jacket on and I was wearing a grey hoodie. I can't remember what Wilson was wearing.

Next to the petrol station were some benches, and as we got close we saw there was a gang of skinheads there. They started shouting at us and someone chucked a beer bottle. It landed right next to me. They were much older, and there were more of them too – probably about ten or fifteen. We picked up the pace, but one of the gang ran after us shouting, 'Wait, wait!'

Me and Wilson carried on walking, but for some reason Jimmy stopped. I think me and Wilson had just gone into the shop when the guy attacked. We heard it, or rather we heard the foot making contact with Jimmy. Jimmy was a wrestler and at the time was Swedish youth champion, so he took the skinhead down and started kicking his head in good and proper on the ground. The guy stayed down and went limp. This caught the attention of the rest of the guys on the bench. They sprinted towards Jimmy, who pegged it inside the shop. My heart was thumping on my chest and you could feel how nervous we all were. Me and Jimmy held the door as hard as we could, whilst the skinheads tried to jog and pull it from the other side.

'Lock it! Lock it!' I shouted.

'I can't,' screamed Wilson.

I realised we wouldn't hold out much longer. A moment later and they managed to force the door. Jimmy ran over to the woman at the till, who looked terrified.

'Get out of here!' he shouted to her, but she was paralysed by fear. Jimmy jumped over the counter to protect her. A few seconds later a guy came up behind him and smashed two bottles over his head. I saw it out the corner of my eye so grabbed two bottles from a fridge and gave the skinhead the same in return. They were glass and contained chocolate milk. The light brown liquid ran over the floor and mixed with the blood from Jimmy and his attacker's heads. Everything was chaos. I remember kneeing somebody and head-butting someone else as I slid around in the mess on the floor. Wilson grabbed hold of a big guy and held him, and I smacked him as hard as I could. It felt kind of absurd, like we were in a film. Bottles and food flew through the air and we fought the skinheads off for a few minutes more before the cops finally pitched up.

The whole petrol station was a wreck and I could hardly walk after using my knee on two guys. That didn't bother me that much though – the worst part was that none of the guys who had started it ended up in the cells. Neither did any of our lot. It was just me, because I smashed those two bottles of chocolate milk over the head of the guy who took on Jimmy. The police saw me and addressed me as Ove straight away. I was only fourteen but the cops already knew the nickname well enough. When it came to the trial later, the guy whose head I had gone for turned it on for the judge and started crying in the courtroom. I had to pay 15,000 - 16,000 kronor in damages to him. I could have not hit him, of course, and let him carry on at Jimmy, but that isn't how it works.

That was what most of the fights I was in looked like. I was always drawn in, but never sought them out. The thing is, if you keep ending up in that type of situation it makes you angry inside. At first Mum would ring the parents of the person I had been fighting to talk about what had happened. Everyone knew that I could not be solely to blame for everything. I mean, everyone was at it, but for some reason I was always the fall guy. It was always Ove.

A week or so later, Jimmy, Wilson and a few other guys ended up in trouble again. A gang from Eskilstuna, which is fairly close to Arboga, had come to town looking for a fight. Police from Örebro and Västerås were drafted in to deal with it. Had they arrived five minutes later, it could have turned out really badly. The Eskilstuna gang had brought chains, and Jimmy, Wilson and me got back-up from mates with baseball bats and axes. A few days later Jimmy called me. I was out somewhere with Antonio at the time, but Jimmy said he had run into a few of the Eskilstuna guys in town and now they were following him.

'We're on our way,' I told him, and when we finally saw him from the safety of Antonio's car he was surrounded down by the local Red Cross office. Me and Antonio jumped out of the car, but as soon as we got there someone hit Antonio straight in the balls. Someone pulled a knife on me, too. I went back to the car, got a screwdriver out of the glove box and went at them. I can't remember any details, only that I had tunnel vision. The guy with the knife tried to take me on, so I sliced his head with the screwdriver.

By the end of that summer I had been hauled up on seven assault charges. School had reported me twice in the spring, and the rest of the charges were fights in town during the holidays. When social services came to the farm to talk to Mum about the assault charges it was a bolt out the blue. Not for me but for Mum, who had no idea about half the fights. I sat next to her in the kitchen as the social worker laid out all the facts. She was angry and sad at the same time.

'How is this possible?' she said. 'Why am I only being told now?'

When I look back on it, I can understand her shock. The first time the police are involved they are supposed to tell social services and then the parents. Whatever the details, it ended up in court and I was convicted of assault in all seven cases, ending up at Sunbo Young Offenders' Home near Fagersta, north of Arboga. To begin with they put me in Aspen, the secure unit. I didn't really care whether I was locked up or not, but for Mum, Kalle and my sisters it was an important difference. The looks from other people in town must have been tough for them to deal with.

Inside Aspen I started fighting immediately. I wanted to borrow a pen to write to Dad, but they said no. It was all I needed to kick off.

I ended up in solitary confinement. I was totally naked. There was no furniture. If I needed to go for a piss there was a drain in the floor. The problem was, putting someone like me in solitary had no effect at all. I only got more aggressive, and more angry. Even today I can't see why they did it. I was fourteen years old and was just locked away. There was no reason to do that.

When Mum found out she started sending letters to the prison service and Thomas Bodström, the Justice Minister. First she demanded to know how they could even think about putting a teenager in isolation, but then she tried to appeal the decision itself. She later admitted that she expended so much energy on me that my sisters were almost forgotten about. Mum, Kalle and Grandma tried everything to help me, but they got nothing for their efforts.

I had already begun to cut myself off. It was like I didn't give a shit about my own future, and I didn't see that what I did also affected them.

Later I was moved to a place called Persbo for rehabilitation. It was a slight improvement. Even if it felt like we were locked away in cold storage and given no chance to learn or change, there was at least the opportunity to fish. I have always liked fishing. Mum and my sisters came to visit as often as they could, and Mum brought tackle and gear with her. She also smuggled in a mobile so I could ring her if I needed anything. I told her it was like being found with a ticking bomb. If they discovered it then I would suffer. Luckily it remained my secret.

After nine months I was released. That same night I went to Eskilstuna with a few mates: Domiku, Darko and Stenvik. He was much older, around twenty-eight, I think. We were in Eskilstuna because Darko had been arguing with his girlfriend, who lived there, and he was adamant he needed to see her. Back then there was a club in town called Blå where everyone went. We parked the car outside and went in. For some reason nobody was getting their ID checked, so we went right up to the bar and started drinking. We were having fun, except for Darko, who spent the entire night trying to ring his girlfriend. Eventually he got hold of her and asked where she was. She said she was at home, but soon afterwards Darko glimpsed her across the club in the company of some other guys.

'What the fuck!' he shouted and ran over. We followed. There were a lot of words exchanged and then suddenly it kicked off. A couple of the guys went for Darko and Domiku. The bouncers tried to stop it, but they didn't stand a chance. Everything happened so fast, and Darko's girlfriend and the other guys made a quick exit. They jumped into a car parked next to ours. We reached it just as they had managed to start the engine. I had been calm the whole time, but now I lost it. I jumped on the bonnet and smashed the windows with my hand. Domiku and Darko dragged out the guy behind the wheel. The bouncers had followed us out but they stood back and watched. They didn't fancy the fight.

We dragged the others out, too. It was total chaos. Someone kicked in several of the driver's ribs. Someone else jumped on the head of one of the other passengers. Then I heard Darko shout.

'Shift it!' he said. I turned around to see a police car turn into the car park with flashing blue lights. We ran. The police car came after. In the nick of time we made it over a fence. We didn't stop until we were well outside town.

Once we were sure we had shaken off the cops Jimmy rang a guy he knew in Arboga and asked him to come and get us. When he arrived we lay on the floor of the car and he zigzagged back home to avoid the police. Luckily that fight never troubled the legal system. We all created alibis for each other, and Darko told his girlfriend, 'Testify against us and you'll make a problem for yourself.'

A few days later Jimmy and me spent the evening at my cousin Adam's watching a film. He had his own house near the station in Arboga. Suddenly Jimmy got bored of the film, or maybe he was a bit restless, but he went and stood at the open door to the street. Me and Adam turned off the film and went out to join him. Just then two girls came walking down the street and Jimmy perked up.

'Alright, ladies!' he shouted.

The girls stopped walking and came over to the house. Jimmy chatted away, and once he had ushered them into the house, he said, 'Well, girls, how about undressing for us, eh?'

'No,' they answered.

'Aw, c'mon!' said Jimmy.

'You get undressed, then we'll do it, too,' they replied.

I looked at Jimmy and felt on edge. As I said, I was shy around girls, had low self- esteem and was not the chatty type.

Jimmy began to take off his clothes.

'Not like that!' they said. 'You have to dance as you do it!'

Jimmy put on some music and began to strip.

'Come on!' he said, looking at me.

'Fuck, I hate you, man,' was all I could muster, before I reluctantly began to take my top off.

When we were standing entirely naked in front of the girls, Jimmy said it was their turn.

'Nah, I think we'll go home now,' they said. They left the house giggling.

It was about this time that Mum got Elina a flat on a street called Herrgårdsgatan in Arboga. Elina had been moaning for ages that she was tired of living so far out of town, and Mum gave in. It meant that every Wednesday, Friday and Saturday it became a party venue. In truth, we totally destroyed the place.

The most damage we ever did was on New Year. The evening started out fine enough and there were a few of us listening to music and joking about. Suddenly Elina's landline rang. Elina was at another party, so I answered it, and on the other end were two guys from the floor below who fancied insulting someone. They talked a whole load of shit about Elina, then they demanded to speak to her.

'Sorry, no,' I said.

They insisted, 'We want to talk to your sister, man.'

But Elina wasn't there. Even if she had been, I wouldn't have let them chat to her.

'Forget it,' I said, and put the phone down. I went back in to join the others. After a while they rang back, so I sighed and told them to get lost. When they rang a third time I left the apartment, went down one floor, and banged on their door. The thing was, by this point it was well known in Arboga that I could fight a bit, and people would go out of their way to provoke me.

The guy in the flat downstairs was called Viktor, and he was the one who opened the door. His mate grabbed my hoody and pulled it over my head so I couldn't see. Then Viktor kicked and hit me as hard as he could. I ended up on my back, but still got away a kick right in the balls on one of them. By the time I managed to get my hood off, I was raging. It looked like Viktor had been on the other end of the kick, because he was bent double. I took the opportunity to attack the other guy before both of them vanished back inside and locked the door.

I was on the way up to my sister's again when I heard them coming back for more. I glanced over my shoulder and noticed they had iron piping. I ran into the flat and locked up behind myself, but they started smashing at the door with the pipes until it broke. It got pretty tumultuous, and when the police arrived I ended up being arrested again. Luckily a friend of Elina's had rung her and warned her before she came home. The outer door hung at an angle and was full of holes. Inside the flat the toilet door had been ripped off, including the whole frame. All Elina's CDs were spread across the floor. On the balcony there were splinters of glass and an axe.

If someone tried to provoke me today, the same way Viktor and his mate did, I would probably let it slide. I'm a totally different person now. Back then I was emotional, and the strongest emotion was hatred. However you look at it or try to dress it up, hate breeds hate and violence breeds violence. Now I loved to fight, of course, and I've always seen the fight itself as something to enjoy. To claim otherwise would be a lie. I would enjoy fighting, or the feeling afterwards, when I had floored a couple of guys and come out on top.

What you have to realise is that I was never the kind of guy to start on innocent people in town. The people I fought were either gangsters or fight junkies like myself. At the end of the day I was deeply insecure. Fighting was the only thing I felt I was really any good at.

Chapter 3
Lads

lmost everyone in the area knew who I was. More accurately, they knew who Ove was. And they were scared of him.

I began to feel worse and worse. I didn't see it then, but now I realise I was climbing further and further into darkness. I was cut off and detached, but internally I was conflicted. My mates would stay over in my cabin on the farm in Boda, or in the flat Mum got hold of for me in Arboga. I was evicted after only a few weeks. It was social services who thought I should live in the flat and take care of myself, but it didn't work. All we did was smoke hash or have parties that always got out of control. My mates said I slept badly and would let out weird sounds. It wasn't that surprising. Everyone in my family was sad and disappointed about my behaviour. They had given me everything and I had gone and ended up like that.

Sure, Mum was an old rockabilly and was a bit crazy when she was younger. She used to fight, too. She recognised the wildness in me, because somewhere it was in her as well. It meant that not just me but my mates could relax around her. But now it had become so serious that even Mum was brought down by it. Even though I had started to cut myself off, it still got to me. Everyone in the area knew who I was. More accurately, they knew who Ove was. And they were scared of him. I was rarely the one to start the fights, but it was more often than not me who had to step in and end them. I did it because I could.

Although I am not much of a team player, I have always liked having a lot of mates around me, and at that time there were probably ten or so of us regularly hanging out together. Several of them have defied the odds and done well for themselves, and I have always asked myself what it was that meant I survived the way I did. Maybe it was because I never really got into drugs. I smoked hash and tried E and coke, but it did nothing for me. I got my kicks elsewhere.

Even today I can tell straight up whether or not someone is a troublemaker. It is an instinct. If you've been one yourself, you recognise it in others. Whatever happened between us, there was always loyalty and respect. You never attacked anyone old or weak,

33

it wasn't what you did. Neither did you attack girls. There were principles. We were just a gang of dropouts who should have been given help, and in many cases needed taking care of.

However bad it got, we looked out for each other. The philosophy was that when we were together, everyone should feel welcome. If someone in Arboga was an outcast then we invited them to hang out with us. Everyone had the right to be who they were and to wear the clothes they wanted to wear. If we saw someone was down, we didn't take the piss out of them. We danced and wreaked havoc, but we didn't just sit on the sofa drinking. Neither did we tell people, 'you can only bring one friend'. We were open to anyone.

We used to hang out with each other's families, too, and though the adults knew we weren't God's most well-behaved children, we were allowed to eat as much as we wanted. Some of the mums would even make us food in the middle of the night. In some families it was different and you were expected to wait in their room when the family had dinner, but home in Boda . . . we could turn up with fifteen lads and lay waste to the fridge. We ate everything in sight.

Jimmy had not lived at home since he was thirteen. He moved about between different mates and their families. In those days he was living with a guy we knew called Mendez, who was extremely thin and had super-thick glasses, because to all intents and purposes he was blind. He also had osteoporosis, flapped about and almost always had something broken. He had balls, though, and fought like a man carrying a hundred kilos of muscle. Every Monday we would go with him to the optician and solder together his glasses, which always broke in the middle when he got in a fight. Mendez was a real character, flouncing about in his hip-hop clothes, cap and jam-jar glasses.

Sometimes we would run into the skinheads, rockabillies or other gangs. Because I was tall and blond I was the most visible of us, which also meant I was the one people would name in witness statements. Even when I wasn't involved, the police would turn up and ask after Ove. One time me, Antonio and Mendez were sat at a pizzeria in Arboga called Fellini. We had kicked off the evening with a bit of vodka. Because we had nowhere to go we went to the station and hung out on the platform. Suddenly Mendez started dancing right there by the tracks. He was particularly amusing when he danced, because his body appeared to lack any bones or muscles. 'Do the chicken dance!' we shouted, or 'Do the frog dance!', and Mendez did a whole load. Perry, another guy who had come out with us, had a camera and filmed everything.

We were on the platform for several hours drinking, and a few of us toked on some joints as well. I think we might have had some kind of dance competition and Mendez did all his dances: the African dance, the ninja dance and the rest.

After a while we decided to go to the pizzeria. The place wasn't big. There were maybe fifty people in there and it was rammed. We ran straight into the hockey lads and it all kicked off. Someone smacked Antonio, and then it escalated. It just exploded; plates flew, pizza was thrown, windows were broken, while Perry filmed and filmed. One of our crowd, Danne, had an old-style bottle with a heavy bottom. I was by the door and saw him swing it straight into the skull of a boy, who started spurting blood all over the pizzeria. I think Danne must have cracked his head wide open. 'You fucking ragheads!' someone screamed. Perry was a bit away from me filming and shouted, 'That's racial discrimination that is!' It was all caught on film. When the rest of us withdrew, Perry was still standing there with the camera in his hand.

The police arrived a few minutes after we had gone. Perry told me later that the first thing they asked was whether I was there. The second thing they asked was whether I had been there. They were convinced it was me who had split that guy's head wide open. Perry said it wasn't, so they took him in and confiscated the film as evidence. Apart from seeing the proof of who had really put the bottle into the guy's skull, they presumably also got a laugh from watching Mendez do the chicken dance on the station platform.

One of the few times the police never came looking for me, even though I had been fighting, happened a few days later. I was stood outside the same pizzeria waiting for my mates. They were older than me and that night the security guy was checking ID, so I didn't get in. After a while outside this guy came over. He was about thirty, and for the story we can call him Pelle.

'You're a real wannabe black, aren't you?' he said.

'What?' I said, hands in my pockets. 'What the fuck are you on about?'

'You're such a fucking little wannabe black guy, eh?' he repeated and looked around, aiming a punch at my head as hard as he could. I had time to duck and pulled my hands out of my pockets, planting two blows right on his mouth. He stumbled backwards and landed on a bike rack. I jumped on top of him and let him have it. The pavement was crowded with people, and out of the corner of my eye I saw Domiku and Danne come out of the pizzeria.

At the same moment two of Pelle's mates came over and took a hold of me. Domiku and Danne came at them. There was a proper fight and people on the street formed a ring around us. After a while this old rockabilly drove his car straight through the crowd and me and Pelle ended up on the bonnet. I gave Pelle a good seeing to. When I was done, he had no front teeth left. Pelle never reported me to the police. He would go on to lead a motorbike gang for a while, and today he has a photo of us together as his Facebook image, standing with our arms around each other.

Of all the stuff that happened when I was growing up there are some things I regret more than others. One such occasion was midsummer 2004. Mum had been moaning at me, or rather pleading with me, to stay in Boda and not go into town, because she was afraid I would end up in a fight, same as always. After a while I gave in, and that afternoon a whole load of us went down to the meadow in Sundänge, where the celebrations were held. It was a recreational area with a load of summer cabins near the Västlandasjön Lake. We had drunk a fair bit and had fun. Towards evening everyone else decided they wanted to go into town, and it was just me, Jimmy, and another guy called Mehmet left behind.

We started walking aimlessly towards the water. Down at the pier we saw a really hot girl who was swimming with another guy. At first we thought he must be her boyfriend, but then we somehow worked out he had to be her brother. Maybe we overhead them talking about it. Anyway, we lay down on the pier and Jimmy and Mehmet chatted while I looked at this girl, trying to make contact. I think I asked what her name was, that kind of stuff. She wasn't the least bit interested, and after a while she and her brother pulled themselves up onto the pier to dry off.

When they were done the brother looked at me and said I'd taken his cigarettes. I don't even smoke, and never have done, so I told him someone else must have. The guy was adamant it must have been one of us. I looked at Jimmy, who didn't smoke either, and asked. Jimmy shook his head, and when I asked Mehmet, he said he hadn't done it. The guy was drunk and gave me a push.

'Give me my fags,' he said.

'Don't touch me,' I replied, pushing him back.

He went for me. At the same time the girl smacked me as hard as she could with a branch in the back. I brushed her off with one hand and thumped the guy in the head like a man possessed. I even carried on when he was on the ground and rolled him down to the edge of the water. He let out a whimper and the girl started screaming like crazy. People quickly ran over, wondering what had happened. Me, Jimmy and Mehmet made a run for it, going all the way through the woods until we reached a road. We ran into some of our neighbours, and walked calmly home as if nothing had happened.

It turned out that Mehmet had actually taken the cigarettes, even though he promised me he hadn't. It took a while, but I forgave him for it.

When we walked into the kitchen the following morning, Mum was sat down. She just looked at us. She had the morning paper in front of her, and after a while she asked, 'What did you get up to last night?'

'Nothing much,' I replied.

'Don't lie to me, what did you do last night?'

Me, Jimmy and Mehmet all looked at each other.

'Did you do this?'

She held up the paper so we could see. It was an article about an assault. I felt terrible, and I reckon Jimmy and Mehmet did too.

'If it turns out that you are behind this, then I never want to see you again. You can all get the hell out of my life,' she said, leaving the kitchen.

We ate breakfast in silence. Then we went into town to meet Domiku, Björn and a few other mates at an apartment, where they sat about drinking. On midsummer day it was tradition to head out to one of the barns in the country and have a party. Jimmy was in touch with this girl called Jessica by text and she asked if we wanted to join her. Nobody fancied it, except Jimmy, who had found some more energy.

'Come on, there'll be girls there,' he said.

Not long after, there were six of us sat in a car on the way to the barn, which was west of Medåker. In front of it was a big lawn, where people were spread out in groups drinking as we parked the car and got out. Everyone stared at us. Music boomed out from the barn, and though I didn't know why, I had a bad feeling as we went up the steps to the top floor to find the bar. The girl Jimmy had been talking to and a mate of hers were there. We went over to say hi, but it was a perfectly sprung trap.

Immediately we found ourselves face to face with a whole bike gang. There were twenty or so of them, in their mid-thirties with the waistcoats and shit. I heard a bang behind me and turned around to see Domiku, who weighed 120 kilos, thud onto the bar. We got out of there quick, taking the steps back down onto the lawn. There we bumped into more bikers, as well as Lars, a lad we had given a beating to several times in the past, but who had suddenly got himself a leather jacket and an attitude.

'You fucking ragheads, what the hell do you want?' he screamed.

I was properly going by this point and shouted back, 'Come over here Lars! Come here so I can kill you!'

Lars took a step back and another guy came forward. He had a shaved head, a chain in his hand, and looked like the gang leader. The bikers from the bar had also made it down. The girl who had tricked us into coming was nowhere to be seen.

The guy with the shaved head shouted something and rushed forward. As he did I stuck out my hand and gave him a precise uppercut. He fell to the ground, and our boys started to kick him. I could feel the adrenalin pumping.

'Anyone else wants a piece of me?' I shouted.

Everyone stood frozen to the spot.

Mendez, Jimmy and Björn also started to shout, 'Come on boys! You started it, how about finishing?'

One of them took the bait and came up to me.

'OK,' I said, 'shall we dance?'

The guy did not say or do anything. Instead he looked at his feet and went back to join the others.

Even if you have a whole gang, it doesn't mean you always have the balls. Often one of them does and the rest are only hangers-on. If you can see the ballsy one is lying in a heap on the ground, then it probably seems less fun.

We moved towards them and they began to back off. There were thirty of them and they were twice our age, but they backed off! We shouted at them, and called them stuff. Then we got back in our car and drove to Mehmet's.

'Shit, guys', said Jimmy, as we stood in his hallway. 'I had a fucking weird dream. I dreamed there were cops waiting outside the apartment.'

'Come on,' we said, 'you're taking the piss now.'

'No man, it was so real. The police were outside the door waiting to cuff us.'

'Chill out,' said Mehmet, 'that won't happen.'

'Nah, 'course not,' said Jimmy. 'Was just a dream, like.'

Chapter 4
Fuck the World

They gave me a year and three months in prison in Kristianstad. It was high security, with three fences of different heights, and the people inside were hard-core criminals.

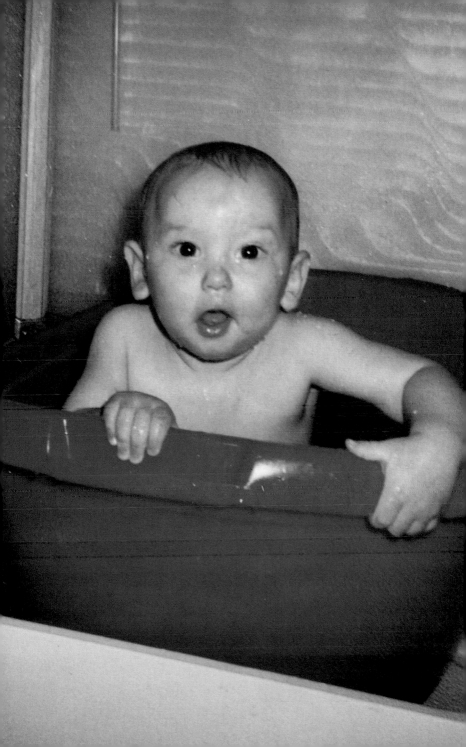

Sitting with my mum — who is holding Elina — and our dog Zack, when I was a boy.

Me and my grandmother.

Visiting the Eskilstuna Zoo as a child.

A shot of me and Mum.

A photo of my dad taken on New Year's Eve 2014.

Me and the guys.

A recent shot of me with Wiggo.

Wiggo and Perra in my gym in Sörby.

Having fun with Perra.

A shot of me and some of my friends from back home.

My Halloween and victory party in Arboga, November 2010.

Whatever I did, and wherever I was, it felt as if I always ended up in the shit regardless . . . as if everything was just fate. I was totally lost. I had no dreams, no goals, no idea about what to do with my life. I was also a wanted man, with arrest warrants hanging over me for the fight with the girl's brother at the lake and, unbelievably, for the showdown with the bike gang.

If I had to draw something positive from my teenage years, it was the fact I reached rock bottom and managed to pull myself up again. I know how it feels when the dark is all you can see.

Ever since I first met him, Antonio has always meant a lot to me. Nowadays we are like two brothers, as he is together with my sister Elina. Back then we hung out and one day went to the tattoo parlour to get identical neck tattoos. We both got *FTW*, which meant *Fuck The World*. That was pretty much how we felt around then. Today the tattoo is a reminder of what it was like in those days, and of everything we went through together.

The tattoo on my chest shows my first dog, Tequila, who I got at the start of that same summer and is gone now. I mention it now because I used to walk her through town for exercise. It was warm out and I had just taken off my shirt when I noticed I was being followed by a green Volkswagen Passat. I carried on walking and the car drove slowly behind. After a while it stopped. Two guys jumped out and ran up behind me.

'Are you Alexander Gustafsson?' they asked.

I remember hesitating. Maybe because I wasn't used to being addressed by my real name. It was really only family who used it. Eventually I nodded.

They were plain clothes cops and told me to get into the car. Then they drove me and Tequila to the jail in Köping. They already had Mehmet, and Jimmy had his freedom another week before they got him. Mum came and took the dog the same day. I sat there for three months in that prison, six weeks of it without privileges. I don't know why I was there so long, but I guess all the interrogations and paperwork must have taken a while. It is a long time to be locked up, especially if you're as restless as I am. Eventually I was given a trial for what had happened by the lake in Sundänge.

Me, Mehmet and Jimmy were all taken straight from jail with our hands cuffed. I remember how angry I was. The girl, her brother and the parents were sat a bit away from us. It turned out they had been in their summer cabin over the holidays. The mother was in tears and said they never wanted to go back after what had happened. I couldn't make sense of it – the idea that we had ruined things for them as much as we had. I looked back on it sometimes and felt guilty, but right then I was angry with the family and the whole stupid trial. The next hearing didn't make me any happier, the one with the biker boss. He was there together with his wife, and he broke down in tears at several points. It struck me as shameful, and more than anything else dishonourable. He was twice my age and had been the one who started it.

They gave me a year and three months in prison in Kristianstad, Jimmy and Mehmet were not convicted. It was high security, with three fences of different heights, and the people inside were hard-core criminals. I was in the young offenders wing for prisoners between eighteen and twenty-five. I was the youngest, and I'm not exaggerating when I say it was fucking tough. There was a wing there for sex offenders. They were the ones who did all the cooking, and soon it was open warfare between us. We gave them stick and they spat and pissed in our food. For some reason the others in our wing decided to nominate me for chairman of the prisoners' representative council. There was a vote. I've said it before and I'll say it again: locking people up does not make them less violent or less criminal. The opposite in fact. There ended up being so much fighting that the staff called me in.

'You're in charge of the prisoners' council,' they told me.

I sighed and said something to the effect of, 'but I haven't fucking done anything'.

'Well, this is how it is,' they said, 'either resign from your position or we put you in solitary confinement.'

I had no wish to spend more time locked up by myself, so when I got back to the others I said, 'Do what the fuck you like, you can get yourself a new chairman.'

They got that the staff had threatened me, so it was all fine. Well, that isn't quite true. After a few months I felt so terrible I was close to giving up. I lost all hope for myself and my future. It was around Christmas when I rang Mum, who I hadn't seen for six months, and told her, 'I can't do this any more. I want to kill myself.'

'But Alex, don't say that!' she tried to comfort me. 'There must be something positive to focus on.'

'There isn't. I can't see a way out.'

'You can't think that way. I'm coming to see you.'

The following day she and two of my sisters really did come and see me. It is almost 500 kilometres from Arboga to Kristianstad, so Mum had driven on icy roads through the night.

I had booked them a visiting room and with the twenty kronor I had to my name, I got some biscuits and Fanta. Mum and my sisters had to be stripped to their underwear and searched before they were allowed in to see me. It was horrible for them, but more than anything else it was humiliating. The visiting room where we spent the few minutes we had together was small. The walls were painted hospital green and covered in filthy graffiti. We sat on a bunk as the room lacked chairs and tables. Next door a psycho was screaming his head off.

We chewed on the biscuits and drank the Fanta the guard had brought in. Mum and my sisters just cried. Even so, it meant the world to me that they had come. It was them and my dog – whose pictures I had on the cell wall – who got me through my time inside there.

For the final three months I was to be moved to an open unit in Botkyrka, near Stockholm. After evening roll-call, me and a few others rolled up a prison blanket, folded it over the barbed-wire fence around the place, and went into town to kick back and relax.

We would always come back for morning roll-call and we stank of alcohol, but as long as we made it on time nobody seemed to mind. Botkyrka didn't mean a change towards more help or treatment either – it was simply a place to keep criminals and somewhere they could meet and socialise with one another. The only plus was that I was assigned a probation officer who I could meet regularly for chats. I have forgotten her name, but she would play a key role in my life. She was also the one who helped me leave that place earlier than planned, electronically tagged.

I still had absolutely no idea what to do with my future. I only knew I had to get away from Arboga and the destructive spiral I found myself in. In prison this thought had started to grow on me that I might go and join the Foreign Legion, and as soon as I got home to Boda, I talked to Mum about it. She understood how important it was for me to get away from everything, so before I had even finished explaining my plan, she said, 'I'll help you, Alex.'

The next day I had contacted the Foreign Legion in Marseille and Mum booked me a one-way ticket.

It was summer and I had to be tagged until 14 July. We were supposed to celebrate Kalle's fiftieth birthday the day after, and then I would leave. That was what me and Mum agreed, anyway.

When I was in Kristianstad, Grandma had done all she could to find a priest who would be able to give me Holy Communion and pray for me. The problem was, because everyone knew about Farmer Ove by this point, it was not straightforward. Eventually she had got hold of a guy called Wiggo Karlsson from the Methodist church, via a friend who organised prayer chains. He took care of junkies and young guys in Köping who needed help, and together with some friends of his ran an organisation called Kontakt from a basement office. Kids could go there to drink coffee and get spiritual care. He was in his seventies, and had devoted his life to Jesus at the age of twenty-five. Since then he had touched not a drop of alcohol, nor a woman. It wouldn't be an exaggeration to say that he did everything he could to help others and went so far – including helping all the addicts and criminal kids – that he was actually banned from preaching in church.

I can remember Grandma being surprised when I agreed to go along. But for me it was an obvious choice. She had been there for me through thick and thin. I had always been able to ring her if something happened. She had picked me up countless times when I'd been drunk or up to something. Once she even hid me from the police.

When we went down to Kontakt a few days later, it felt like I was giving something back for once.

Wiggo had spread out some white cloths, had lit candles and made the whole place really nice. I remember the first thing he asked was, 'Can I have your autograph?'

'Why?' I wondered.

'Well, you'll be a world champion one day.'

I didn't know what to think, but because Wiggo had passed me a slip of paper and a biro, I wrote my name.

Wiggo smiled and posted it up on the wall. It stayed there until the day he died.

I could tell immediately there was something special about Wiggo and that I liked him. He didn't judge me for what I had done. He listened to what I had to say and was interested when I told him what I had gone through. He didn't read from a book when he dished out advice, he just said what he thought. It was simple and clear. When I took Communion with my tag on, Grandma stood beside me in tears.

Me and Wiggo would grow close, and before me and Grandma went home that day, I told him that I was going to Marseille to join the Foreign Legion. Wiggo smiled again. 'God has cancelled the trip,' he said.

I thought it a weird thing to say. Mum had already bought the plane ticket and I was totally set on going. I didn't think any more about it until a few days later, when Kalle turned fifty. It was the day after they took off my tag and two days before I was due to fly to France.

There were loads of people at the party. Grandma had made venison steaks and for once everything felt right. I had arranged to meet up with some of my mates in town later that evening, as we had a friend who also had a birthday that day. Halfway through the party I found Mum and told her I had to go see them.

'Please, don't, just don't,' she said. 'I'm begging you.'

'Take it easy,' I said. 'I'm only popping by.'

An hour or so later I was at Vinbäcken, a pub in Arboga, with the lads. Almost straight away we got in an argument with some guy. Everything happened so quickly. The guy had made a move and before I knew it I had given him an uppercut hard enough that he passed out. Everything stopped. I felt a cold shiver run through me. Then the police arrived.

Mum didn't find out what had happened until the next day. Two officers came out to the farm to tell her. My sisters and our cousins were home. The police asked one of my sisters, Erika, where Mum and Kalle were. She said they were out in the field, and so they went to find them. I have no idea how they reacted to the news, but when Grandma heard she screamed. After a few days in custody I got a letter from Mum, and I'll never forget what she wrote: *Alex, I can't go through all of this again. You're in God's hands now.*

Mum had never written or said anything like that to me before. She had shouted at me, got angry, been upset and smacked me round the ear. But now she had given up on me. She wrote that I had to choose my own path, and that she could no longer be there by my side to support me. The letter finished with: *I'll see you when I see you.* I read it several times and each time it felt as if something broke inside me. She had cut herself off and it hurt. What hurt most was the realisation of what I had done to her and all the others close to me.

That feeling of fate playing its hand hit me again; the feeling that I was destined to lead a life of crime. Now it is time to go all in, I said to myself. I had messed up. I could have left. I could have not fought back. But I am a fighter. I was also always the one pushed forward when it got heavy. That's no excuse, though, and I can't dodge the blame or push it onto someone else, because it was a role I happily took on.

At the trial things went the same way as they had done so many times before. I told the room my story, but the judge took the other guy's side totally. That wasn't maybe so unreasonable, as I was drowning in convictions. There was a whole wodge of papers there, so they had virtually no trust in what I said. I was also classified as extremely dangerous. I had cuffs on, but there were two policemen in the room itself keeping a constant eye on me. Nobody apart from Grandma had come from my family to watch the trial. It used to be that I would plead innocent. Then I just told the judge, 'I confess to everything. Do what you have to with me.'

I was on early release, meaning I actually still had half a year to serve on my last sentence. I reckoned I would get at least two and a half then.

However, the probation officer I had met several times during the last few months in Kristianstad was at the trial. Suddenly she got up and told the judge, 'If you put him inside again, you'll see him back here soon enough. He needs care and treatment.' I remember how committed she was when she spoke. She said that I was only nineteen and still not set in my ways. That kind of stuff. Then I was taken out of court so the jury and the judge could consider the verdict.

When I came back in, it turned out they had listened to the probation officer's advice. Instead of two years inside I was given the same time at a secure home. Someone from the home was there too. When he came up to me afterwards, I asked with surprise, 'So, I won't be locked up?'

'Trust me,' he answered. 'You'll wish you were locked up. At least that was comfortable. Prison is a walk in the park compared to what happens now.'

I followed him to his car and we went straight to Boda to collect clothes and the other stuff I needed to take with me. Kalle was there and looked really disappointed. We didn't have time to speak to each other, but I could tell by looking at him. Mum and my sisters weren't home.

Chapter 5
The West Coast Family

I looked closer and tried to work out what it was, and the light came slowly nearer. When it was only a few metres away, I thought it looked like a spaceship from a sci-fi film.

The West Coast Family was a turning point for me in so many ways. Apart from the younger guys like me, there were veterans who had done eight or nine years inside and were there for rehabilitation. Then there were the guys with drink and drug problems. This last lot seldom handled the hard-core methods the home used very well and were locked away, but the Family was exactly what I needed.

All the drills and the wake-ups, the cleaning, the food prep and the hard physical training kept me calm. As well as your chores you also had the option of studying for high-school exams. You could even learn to dive. The idea was it taught you how to take care of yourself and others. Most of us had as much of a clue about responsibility as we did about the intended consequences of our rehabilitation exercises. When you dive, you have to depend on your diving buddy. If something happens down there then that person is literally the difference between life and death.

I had never dived before, but physical challenge has always got me going. When diving presented just such a challenge, I was away.

The idea was that those of us who had chosen diving would end up with a diving certificate. If you wanted you could then use it to go on and become a diving instructor. It was not only about finding a way back into society, but about getting that feeling of achievement when you realise you have done something.

Carlos, who I had become mates with, was one of the instructors and held the first preliminary lesson. Me and Carlos were training together the whole time, and after the lesson he waved at me and said, 'I know a guy renovating an aikido club in Stockholm. I used to train there. We can have all the old equipment if we want it. They've got mats, beanbags and the rest. There's a storeroom in the basement here nobody uses any more. I thought we could start a dojo down there.'

There wasn't any 'if' about it. Carlos hired a little truck and we set off after breakfast the following morning. Then we drove straight up to Stockholm and picked up all the stuff from a place in Östermalm. We were back with the Family that same evening. Over the next few days we emptied the storeroom of rubbish, laid out the mats, repainted, and fixed stuff. When we were done, it was ready for training. We had boxed a fair bit and Carlos must have seen something in me, because he started to push me hard. Every day, like clockwork, we would do the normal morning exercise between half six and half seven, and then another afternoon session around five, when I was done with all my chores and lessons.

Carlos was a big fan of the philosophy behind martial arts. He thought it was something that people had forgotten about. 'It is all technical stuff nowadays,' he said before our first morning session in the dojo. 'In the olden days there was a philosophical element to it, based on the Japanese code of Bushido. Bushido means *way of the warrior,* and a true warrior must learn to die without fear. He must be cold as he stares death in the face.'

'What are you on about? Nobody is going to die here,' I laughed, as I faced him.

'Death can strike at any time.'

Carlos had told me a bit about his childhood, so I knew he was quite an expert on the matter.

'You are exactly like I was at your age,' he said, 'full of anger you don't know how to use. You get yourself caught up in all kinds of shit that just drags you down. You need to learn to channel it, all that energy and rage. You can carry on the same as before and end up with a life sentence after you finally kill someone, or you can choose this path.' He looked around. 'You can become good at it, and it will give you confidence.'

'Let's do it,' I said.

'Great,' said Carlos, 'I'll try and work out what your strong points are so we can develop them. If I'm successful, there'll be no need to prove yourself on the street. It's simple really; don't do to others what you wouldn't want them to do to you.'

That last bit reminded me of the golden rule in Christianity, and it was as if something suddenly fell into place there and then.

'You also have to learn to forgive,' Carlos told me, putting me in a hold and flipping me onto the mat before I had time to blink. He looked at me as I lay on my back and started laughing.

The following day we were due to go to Lysekil on the coast for a week of diving. Autumn had come and there was a chill in the air, but it didn't stop us one bit. After the first night there at the diving centre, we were up and about as early as usual, and we ran the 10K in dry suits, throwing ourselves in at the end. We swam round arm-in-arm and chanted drill songs as we went. Even with the dry suits on we started freezing soon enough, our teeth chattering together. Then we had to familiarise ourselves with the equipment. Diving in the open sea is a totally different ball-game. Some people can't manage it at all. They can be as big and tough as you like on land, but in the water with a tank on their back and visibility of less than a metre, it isn't half as simple.

This was especially true of a gangster who was due to do his first dive with Carlos. The guy must have weighed at least 120 kilos and looked like he'd hit the steroids quite hard through the years. He was covered in tattoos and had a right attitude on him. But when he got in the water, even near the beach, he was struck by panic. He surfaced after no more than a minute with tears in his eyes. It hardly went any more smoothly when he had to do his first proper open-water dive.

We had gone quite far out in the big motorboat, and Carlos and this guy were supposed to dive down to a platform two metres under. Then they were to go to one at five metres, and finally one at seven. Carlos took the guy down to the first platform. So far, so good, but then it got much more challenging. Between that platform and the next the visibility plummeted. By the time they got to the third platform it was almost impossible to see. That was when the big lad started hyperventilating. The panic made him think he couldn't breathe, but in actual fact the precise opposite was true. When you hyperventilate you breathe too much, but he didn't get this. All he wanted was to get back to the surface as quick as possible. The thing is, you can't go straight up in one go. The air in your lungs expands too quickly and you risk dying.

Because this guy was so big, Carlos realised he had no other option than to expel air from his life jacket and lay himself on top. Quite simply, Carlos made himself so heavy that the guy couldn't surface. The guy didn't like it, of course, kicking and flailing wildly. Carlos didn't stop, calmly pushing him down and presumably saving his life at the same time.

When they got back into the boat, it turned out the big guy had shit himself.

Coming up early wasn't only deadly, it could also cost a lot of money. If the divers came up at the wrong speed and hadn't got rid of all the hydrogen, like they were supposed to do, then the dive-team leader had to ring the coastguard and get them to bring a decompression chamber down. You also had to ring the police. It could end up being a very expensive exercise.

The day after the incident with the shit, there was another guy who broke the rules and came up two minutes late from a one-hour dive. In that world two minutes is a long time, and for all we knew he could have been dead on the seabed. This guy had just decided to not surface, and Carlos and the other instructor went mad at him. Because the punishments were collective in the Family, we all got done for it. This was the last dive of the day, but instead of riding back in the boat from the island where we were doing the exercises, we all had to swim back to the diving centre. Seven kilometres in freezing water. We almost froze to death thanks to that idiot. Despite that, I did what I could to keep the others going.

'Keep it up, lads!' I shouted as I swam alongside the group, a few metres behind the boat with the instructors. 'Hurry up so we can get some dinner!'

For me the diving was brilliant. I had to concentrate, and that made me more relaxed and less tense. I liked the night dives, too, which had a really special atmosphere. You can't see a thing outside the torch beam, but there's still movement everywhere. At night everything under the water comes alive. There are crabs, lobsters, starfish and all the other marine life you can think of, up and about looking for food.

It is too much for some people. I was seriously put to the test myself when me and another guy tried our first night dive. We had just got down to thirty metres when our torches suddenly went. It was completely unpredictable, but they went out as if someone had pulled out the plug. Everything was pitch black and you couldn't tell what was up or down. Nor did I know where my partner was in the blackness. My heart began to thud in my temples and my breathing ran away. Suddenly though I felt the loose gravel of the seabed under my feet, so I stood still and tried to breathe normally. I had no idea how much air I had left or how much time was remaining before I was due to surface. I had no idea about anything.

Suddenly I was struck by the strange feeling of being watched. Through my steamed-up goggles I could make out a weak glow of light in the otherwise total darkness. I looked closer and tried to work out what it was, and the light came slowly nearer. When it was only a few metres away I thought it looked like a spaceship from a sci-fi film. It flickered and flashed, revealing a smooth outline. Suddenly I realised it was a little octopus swimming straight towards me. With a thud it collided with my mask. It blinked and looked at me with its huge eyes, its little body shimmering as if it was covered in miniature Christmas-tree lights. Then it did a half turn and vanished back into the darkness, leaving me alone. *Fuck this,* I thought, and took off my weighted diving belt. I pushed myself up and breathed out so there was nothing left in my lungs.

It was against all the rules and really dangerous. I should have gone up in stages to equalise the pressure, but I wanted to get to the surface as quickly as possible. My lungs were squashed as much as they could be at forty metres, when you can hardly breathe and the pressure makes you piss yourself. When I reached the surface I screamed out and took the deepest breath I think I have ever inhaled. A second later my diving partner popped up a few metres from me and made a similar sound.

'What happened?' he asked, when he had got enough air in his lungs to speak.

'My torch went. So did yours.'

As I swam to the boat I wondered if I really had seen an octopus down there. Maybe it had been a hallucination. At that depth when the panic sets in, the mind can play tricks on you.

Onboard we told Carlos what had happened straight away. He was about to go crazy at us for coming up too early, but instead he told us about the first time he had gone down to thirty metres on a night dive.

'It wasn't actually far from here. I went down and waited before turning the torch on so I didn't blind my diving buddy. At thirty metres I switched it on, but I had hardly moved before it went again. It was black as night. I lost my bearings and began to hyper-ventilate. I just wanted to get out, but I knew that it could be deadly. I tried to control my breathing and took deep breaths. Eventually I calmed down a bit and looked around. I saw this faint shimmer of light a little way away and began to swim towards it. There were some other divers there. I grabbed hold of one of their tanks and held on. It was my only chance. The guy didn't seem to notice he had a passenger, as when we reached the surface I heard him say to his mates, "Shit, that was a tough climb!"'

A few days later we were back with the Family. Me and Carlos carried on our intense training in the dojo, and when we were done with the afternoon session, he suddenly asked me a question. 'Ever heard of MMA – Mixed Martial Arts?'

I shook my head and lay down exhausted on the mat.

'I'll show you a few fights. I think it might be your kind of thing.'

Later that night we sat down in the entertainment room, next to the paintball ranges where we would sometimes fight each other, and watched YouTube clips on Carlos's laptop.

'This guy is probably the world's best-ever fighter,' he said, pointing to a stacked white guy climbing into the ring. 'He's Russian, Fedor Emelianenko. His opponent is called Minotauro and comes from Brazil. Until this fight people thought he was unbeatable, but watch what happens.'

I watched and sat open mouthed. It was like nothing I had ever seen before. The Russian was skilful and quick as a cobra, even though he was a heavyweight. When he got the Brazilian on the floor, he got on top of him and unleashed punches in a way that left me breathless.

Carlos showed me a few more of Emelianenko's matches. In one fight he was up against another Brazilian who was at least thirty centimetres taller and looked like a sumo wrestler. Fedor floored him time and time again, finishing with what Carlos termed 'hammer blows'. Another match was won with a wrestling lock and Carlos explained that there were countless ways to win and lose a fight. You could punch your opponent, kick, elbow them, or get a technical knockout where one fighter can no longer defend themselves and the referee has to step in. You could also gain victory through 'submission', where you pinned the other fighter's arms or legs, or choked him until he gave up by banging his hand three times.

A lot of MMA fighters came from Brazil. Carlos said it was because the sport had its roots in Brazilian jiu-jitsu, and showed me a clip of some absolutely insane fighters, Wanderlei Silva and Maurício 'Shogun' Rua.

Silva had been given the nickname 'Axe Murderer' and it was not hard to see why. His style was the most brutal I had ever seen. Shogun was hardly any tamer. He was a black belt in Brazilian jiu-jitsu and seemed able to unleash deadly kicks. Carlos said all the guys we watched competed in Japan for an organisation called Pride.

It was claimed that the Japanese Yakuza were behind it all, 'but this type of business has always attracted criminals,' said Carlos and smiled wryly. 'There's nothing too surprising about that.'

'An American group called UFC has started to take it over,' he continued, 'and they are trying to clean it up and get rid of the bad-boy image. They get that there is a lot of money to be earned if you can make the sport socially acceptable. That's when the crowds and the sponsors will start coming. It wouldn't surprise me if UFC buy up Pride soon enough to get their hands on all the good fighters. That's when it'll become big business.'

We watched a few more fights before I went to bed. I couldn't sleep, though. I was too wired from what I had just watched. MMA was not simply a great sport to watch, it also made me want to climb into the ring. That battle, man against man, drew me in. It had always drawn me, but this was another level. It was more technical, more brutal, and more life and death. There was nowhere to hide.

The next day, me and Carlos began to try out some of the moves we had seen the previous night. Straight away I saw how tough it was, and that a lot of training was needed to get things right. Carlos said after the session he could only take me so far. 'Sure, I can fight, but I don't have a lot of talent, nor do I have the composure you need. I can fight because I have trained hard for years, but you have real talent. You need to hone it. If you do it right you can be the best in the world one day, trust me.'

I stared at him. I was convinced he was taking the piss, but he looked deadly serious. As if he could read my thoughts he said, 'I'm not joking, if you invest in this, then you can go as far as you want to.'

If you behaved and did what you were told at the Family, then after three months you were allowed to go home for a weekend. I had been a good boy and it felt great to travel back and be with my real family and my mates for a few days. When you got back on the Sunday night, however, you had to be clean: no drugs. That was when problems arose. There was a guy who usually never sat still because he had ADHD, or one of the other sets of letters they tick off. He toddled into the office where the staff were signing all the weekenders back in. This guy, who was suddenly totally relaxed, smiled and asked, 'Alright, boys, how's it going?'

'Alright. Yourself?' replied Carlos.

'Great, thanks. Fancy some coffee?'

Carlos got up and grabbed the boy's arm.

'Come with me, you're going to take a piss for us.'

'But I've not done anything,' he protested.

'Then you really have nothing to worry about,' said Carlos and dragged him off.

The urine test showed that the guy had taken amphetamines. That was why he was so chilled. Amphetamines are sometimes prescribed to people with ADHD and similar conditions, but self-medication was not a valid excuse in the Family. As a punishment he had to go outside and land 800 blows on a tractor tyre with a sledgehammer. Then he had to frog-hop ten laps around the building. Given how big it was, it took him a fair while to get it done.

For my part, I was careful to play by the rules when I was given leave. When I got time away for Christmas, I spent it all in the family home. The only exception was Christmas Day, when I went to a party over at Antonio's. He had a niece called Dania, who until then I had always seen as a child, quite simply because she was a few years younger than me. Suddenly she had grown and got some nice curves. I stared at her and she stared back, and soon we were both sat on the sofa with a beer in hand. I felt straight away that there was a spark between us. But man, it was Antonio's niece! I couldn't do anything right under his nose like that. Nowadays Antonio wouldn't have much to argue about, as he went and got together with my sister Elina.

I took Dania's hand and stroked it with my thumb. Then I leaned over and kissed her. Suddenly I felt the mood in the room change and everyone went quiet. Before I even turned my head, I could feel the stare from the other side of the room where Antonio was standing. His eyes were black and his face tight. *Shit, this is going to end badly*, I thought. I had always looked up to Antonio, so it felt terrible when he came over and shouted at me.

'What the fuck are you doing?'

I defended myself by saying she wasn't a little girl any more. Antonio didn't buy it. He carried on shouting and we were close to throwing punches. If a few of our mates hadn't pulled us apart we would have gone at each other for real. I said I thought he was an idiot, and he said I thought I was. I left soon afterwards.

Next day I called Dania and we met up in secret before I went back to the Family. We spoke every day on the phone, and I persuaded her to come down and see me. I managed to smuggle her into my room. Carlos found out, but just laughed and promised not to say anything.

Once me and Dania had been seeing each other a while, I told her that I had to meet her family and ask her dad for permission to be with her. They had apparently found out we were an item, and because my reputation in Arboga wasn't too positive, I didn't think I had much choice.

On my next weekend release, I went to Dania's to speak to them. We sat on the big sofas in her sitting room and drank coffee, looking at each other without saying much. After a while Dania's dad said to me, 'So, you want to date my daughter?'

I nodded, and he sighed and looked at Dania. Then he sighed again and nodded. It was a done deal.

The Family really gave me the structure I needed to feel better and want to go on. I was also back in shape. Instead of being quite chubby – bordering on fat – when I arrived at the home, now I had clear lines on my stomach.

'I know I've said it before,' Carlos told me after training one day in January, 'but you should really put everything into this. Do it right and I promise you, you'll be part of the UFC in two or three years.'

'Ah, get lost,' I told him, throwing my boxing gloves into a corner.

'Hey, maybe I'm not a world champion in anything,' said Carlos, 'but I have a lot of experience, which means I notice certain things. What I see right now is someone custom-made for this who can reach the very top.'

I stood in silence, not knowing what to say.

'Alex . . .' He looked at me seriously. 'I know a guy runs an MMA club in Gothenburg. I want you to go and see him, it'll give you a chance to do something.'

Chapter 6
Gladius

 he guy threw me about like a doll. I found it frustrating, but once he had me down for the seventh time, all I could do was admit I had nothing more to hit him with.

The wet snow whipped me in the face as I walked down the street. I was more nervous than cold. Carlos had arranged permission for me to be away for half a day, so after lunch I took bus 610 by myself from Rävlanda, where the Family was, into Gothenburg. In the hour or so the journey took, I doubted my decision several times. Who did I think I was? Sure, I had boxed and done a bit of fighting on the street, and the last few months I'd trained intensively with Carlos. But this was different, completely different. Even so, as I kicked through the slush looking for the entrance to the club, I was wired. Being nervous and being excited have always gone hand in hand for me. That's where the real kicks are, the ones that make the adrenalin flow and the heart beat faster.

Suddenly I saw a sign saying Gladius over a tiny door from the street.

I walked in through the doorway and found myself in a little reception room, next to a shop with an array of training equipment.

The blonde girl behind the desk smiled at me.

'Are you a member?'

I shook my head and told her the situation, that I had a mate who thought I should try out MMA.

'OK,' she said, still smiling, 'you can talk to one of our instructors and they will be able to assess you.'

The girl pointed to the changing rooms, one floor down.

I went down, changed, and hurried to the gym. Just like in our dojo back at the Family, the air was stale and smelt of leather and sweat. An older butch guy in a tracksuit came over and asked if I was the one who wanted to try out MMA.

I nodded and he took me into one of the rooms, where two guys were wrestling. Once I had warmed up with a skipping rope, the coach told one of them to try and wrestle me. I had done a bit of wrestling with Carlos and this boy was thinner and a head shorter than I was. I thought it would go better than it did. Before I knew what was happening to me he had me on the floor and locked in a hold so I couldn't move. The coach told us both to get up. The same thing happened the second time. And the time after that. The guy threw me about like a doll. I found it frustrating, but once he had me down for the seventh time, pressing my face to the floor, all I could do was admit I had nothing more to hit him with.

Had anyone so much as laughed at what happened, I might never have set foot in the ring again. But none of the boys in the room so much as blinked. The coach said he wanted to see me box instead.

That went better. I kept my opponent at a distance and landed a few nice punches. Then they wanted us to grapple; chokes and different holds on the floor. It was useless. I quickly ended up pinned in an armlock, which I later found out was called a kimura. It felt like my entire arm was going to be ripped off and I screamed in pain.

'That'll do,' mumbled the coach.

I was beaten to a pulp. Everything hurt. Nonetheless, I was anything but broken by the experience. The challenge of learning all the different styles and moves had got me going, and the only thing that worried me was whether the coach would decide I wasn't up to the job.

'We've got space in the beginners' class. Come back tomorrow or on Friday,' he said.

'Of course,' I replied, trying to hide the relief and happiness I felt.

When I had changed and gone back out into the wind and biting snow I was on a high. I walked to the tram stop on Vasagatan, and spent the entire journey back to Rävlanda wondering how I could get the staff back at the Family to approve my day release, so I could carry on training at Gladius. I knew Carlos would stand up for me, but I also needed to persuade the rest of them.

Luckily I had done all my chores and jobs at the home without fault. They had said that I could go soon into the rehabilitation phase in the city. That gave you more freedom, but with that freedom came responsibility. You had to prove you could live a normal life in society, and that meant holding down a job, being punctual, and staying out of trouble. It was the big test before they finally let you go.

As soon as I was back in Rävlanda, I went to find Carlos and explained the situation.

'Amazing!' he said. 'We'll see to it that you can make it to training.'

Next morning I was waiting for him and ready to go outside the dojo when he arrived with a smile on his face.

'Job done!'

It was the best present anyone could possibly have given me, and two days later I was back speaking to the blonde girl behind the reception desk.

'I'm here to join the beginners' class and need to buy a membership,' I said.

From that day on I was addicted. MMA became as important to be as the diving had been. I still planned to carry on diving with Carlos and the others, and to take my certificate in the spring. But it was in the training sessions at Gladius that I felt I had finally found my place. That was where I really came alive.

I trained several times a week, ignoring the fact I had to travel a couple of hours each time to join the training sessions. Soon enough I'd be able to walk to and from the gym, and with spring on the way there'd be no icy wind blowing in from the sea.

There were all sorts of guys amongst us beginners. Who you were didn't matter, though; all of them soon got whipped by me. If I take to a challenge then the learning curve is always quick. Maybe my impatience helped – I couldn't wait to take in as much of the sport as possible, mentally and physically.

At Gladius you were supposed to go one term in the beginners' class. After that there was an advanced group the term after. Once you had done both, you were allowed to move up to high-level stuff in the third term. After that you were finally allowed to be part of the elite group. Only then were you thrust into a real match.

I must have made an impression on my coach, because pretty quickly I was moved from the beginners' class to the elite group of fighters without doing the other two stages. Understandably some of the other lads at the gym got jealous. They gave me dirty looks and I was sure I knew what they were saying behind my back. *Who the fuck does this guy think he is? I could have him any time I like.*

Even back at the Family there were guys who got bitter; I was allowed to travel to and from Gothenburg more or less unrestricted.

'What the fuck does this guy have that I don't?' someone asked.

'Talent,' replied Carlos.

The person who decided I should jump straight to the elite squad was the head coach at Gladius. His name was August Wallén and he was a pioneer of the Swedish MMA scene. He had been Swedish heavyweight shootfighting champion in the nineties, a forerunner to MMA, and August more or less imported it himself from the States.

At the same time another important MMA pioneer came onto the scene with some big foreign influences. Omar Bouiche had been a star fighter of Pancrase, a Japanese fighting syndicate. The name came from ancient Greece, where they had a combat sport called pankration that is a lot like MMA. The ancient Greeks were even more brutal; they hardly had any rules at all. Anything except biting and gouging was allowed, and there was no limit to how long you could go on.

I quickly saw what a leader August was. He led his flock uncompromisingly and shone in both the coach's shoes and in the ring at the showdowns he would organise himself. It wasn't a problem for me, I wanted to get better and, just like Carlos, August saw my talent and told me he wanted to make me into a top fighter. It was only later, when I had finally become one, that things went sour between us. Back then he taught me a lot that I would go on to use. Training with the elite squad was also a great motivator. I mowed down everything in my path and loved it. You can imagine what my opponents thought about it – here I was straight out of kindergarten, and I was sweeping aside guys who had got there the hard way. It didn't help that I scarcely had the ego to match my performances.

If you were in the elite squad, then you could take part in amateur matches. It wasn't only me and Carlos who thought it was exciting. My mates started to show an interest in what I got up to. When I met Jimmy on a weekend release back in Arboga, he said, 'Alex, when you go in for your first fight, I'll be there as sure as I am you'll win it. I'll make it if I'm on my deathbed. I promise.'

He kept his promise, because when he showed up at the martial arts club Stockholm Shoot in the city centre, where the matches were being held, he had a cough and a fever. His nose was a string of mucus.

'Jimmy, you look fucking dead, man!' I said.

'Ah, just a cold,' he said. 'I promised you I'd come.'

'Great, but sit down and take it easy.'

Jimmy just smiled. 'Nail him,' he said, before vanishing off to join the crowd.

When it was time for me to step into the ring, I started to get so nervous that I had tunnel vision. The guy I was up against was called Claes and fought for a team in Uppsala. He looked like a real posh boy and I thought it would be an easy fight. But the butterflies in my stomach had beaten up a hurricane, and I could hardly hear what the ref said as the match got underway.

A second later I blacked out completely. All I know is that Claes floored me with his first punch but that I somehow pulled myself up again. What happened after that is a complete blank for me, to the extent I had to ask the coach afterwards.

'How did it go? What happened? Did I win?'

'Of course you damn well won!' he said, smiling broadly.

Jimmy came running up to me. He appeared to have been cured completely in the space of a few minutes. 'You were amazing!'

'But I can't remember a thing!' I complained.

Jimmy laughed. 'You went at him like a madman. Put him on the floor three times and nearly ripped the ring to pieces,' he said. 'The ref tried to stop you, but it was impossible. Complete chaos but the crowd loved it!'

Only then did it begin to sink in. I had won. I couldn't stop myself swelling up with pride.

'You showed him, Alex,' said Jimmy. 'Trust me, there's a reason you should keep going with this. MMA could be your way out.'

Jimmy was right. This was my big chance. Only a year before, the future had seemed a dead end. It was as if I needed to hit the bottom hard enough to wake me up.

The next match went a similar way, not long after my debut. I needed a whack in the face to get me going. After that it wasn't long before my opponent was finished.

Even though I had won my first two amateur bouts by going at them like a psycho and knocking them out in the first round, I never got ahead of myself. I knew this was only the beginning and that I needed to work hard to take myself higher.

But life was so much better than it had been a year before. Above all else, there were things I really wanted to do.

I wanted to get my diving certificate.

And I wanted to be with Dania.

I wanted to make my final days at the Family as good as the ones already past. The rehabilitation unit I was at in Gothenburg was like living in freedom again.

I wanted to take that final step. Most of all, I wanted to become really, really good at MMA. I was in love with the sport and knew I was made for it. It meant I always looked forward to going to Gladius to train. There was a lot to learn, and now I was on the elite squad I met better opponents. All the same, I pushed aside everyone I came up against. Still, other people got annoyed by it. In their eyes I was an amateur on a lucky roll. Even August began to look at me with a weird stare.

I wasn't as good as him yet. He'd been doing it for years and was a veteran professional fighter, but I felt something about our relationship change when he congratulated me on winning my third fight with a knockout. It was the same hysterical attack, the same tunnel vision as previously, where my mind went blank. Only after I had watched the replays on the computer could I see what I had actually done.

'Jesus, did I do that?' I said, genuinely surprised.

Even if I can't remember much about those early fights, I remember seeing them as gladiatorial battles. It was about beating and subduing an opponent who was there to hurt you. You couldn't expect any mercy. It was life or death, and that meant you had to be as brutal as the other guy.

I won my next two matches as well. That made it five in a row, four of them on technical knockouts. I'd also taken down some professionals in training, guys who fought across the continent.

One day after a boxing session, August called me over.

'This isn't working,' he said.

'What isn't?' I asked.

'This,' he said, pointing to the guy I had just sparred with. 'You keep smashing up all my fighters, and you win every single match. You can't carry on as an amateur any more.'

I laughed, but he shook his head and said, 'I mean it. You should turn pro.'

'OK,' I said, even if I couldn't quite make sense of it. Now I was the kind of person who liked things to move quickly, but I could hardly keep up with myself. The only person who seemed unsurprised by it was Carlos.

'I told you,' he said, slapping me on the shoulder. 'You're born for MMA. You just need to focus and seize the opportunity.'

We were in the boat after one of our many dives. I had passed my diving certificate and could have jumped on a plane to Thailand to work as an instructor once I had been officially released. The

73

thing was, there was a little thing keeping me in Sweden. It was something I felt I had always been waiting for. MMA was a gift, a way to a new life. I also saw the sport as a tool with which I could make Mum and all those I had wronged proud of me again, even if it wasn't a cause for immediate celebration.

'Please, Alex, do you really have to do this?' she would say over the phone. I tried to tell her that it wasn't half as dangerous as it looked. There were more serious injuries in showjumping and ice hockey. She didn't seem to really buy it, though – she was ready to pass out after some of my amateur bouts. All I knew was that fighting was a way to a better life, for me and her. It couldn't be bad that I had finally found something to channel all my energy into, something I was good at.

Every day I waited for news of my first pro match. I tried harder than ever to stop the waiting getting to me, and I thought I was making good progress. Standing was still my best position, but I began to improve at the other stuff as well. At the same time, I realised how far I had to go before I could get close to the skills of the guys fighting in the Pride matches I watched. MMA was a science, and I had barely read the first page of the textbook.

I was so taken up with training that I was genuinely surprised when Carlos came into the gym one day and said, 'How does it feel to know you'll be a free man in two weeks?'

First of all it hit me that I had really no plan for life after the Family. All I had thought about was my training. Dania had said I could move into her dad's place in Hässelby outside Stockholm, where Antonio also stayed. That wouldn't be too bad, I thought, but I had to find a way to support myself and that meant getting a job in Stockholm. I told Dania by phone that night.

The following morning she rang me back.

'I've spoken to Dad, and you can have a job in his building firm.'

'Really?' I said, feeling like everything was falling into place. Gladius already had a partnership with an MMA club in the capital where I could train. It was Stockholm Shoot, where I had fought my first bout. I told August about my plans and asked his opinion.

'Sounds good,' he said.' I'll have a word with them so you can train here and there.'

Then he said, 'Oh, and I've arranged your professional debut.'

'What? For real!'

'November 17th. You'll be fighting at a showcase in Lahti.'

Two weeks later I was ready to leave the Family. Dania had come down to help me pack. It was a quick job, and once we had waved off the van with the stuff in, all we had left to do was get on the train to Stockholm, in an autumn twilight so misty and grey that all the contours of the landscape faded into one another. Even so, I thought the bleak landscape of farms, fields and clumps of trees was beautiful as it raced past.

I took Dania's hand in mine.

Things were just getting going.

Chapter 7
The Road to UFC

You have the right instincts, but we need to improve your technique.

The day of my first pro fight got closer and closer, and naturally I was feeling nervous. However, it gave me a real kick to be able to train at Stockholm Shoot. Sure, the place was a bit run down, in the half-darkness under a concrete transport interchange, and the smell of piss was always there in the background, but the gym itself was well put together and the atmosphere was good.

I made friends easily and got to know several of the other fighters, including Nico Musoke and Martin Machlin, who were about to make their pro debuts like me. I had really good coaches, like Jesper Hallberg, who I think was pretty beaten by the time I finished my first boxing session with him. He looked as if he was in shock after we had gone a couple of rounds together.

'Jesus, are you sure you used to be an amateur?' he asked, as he collapsed onto the ropes.

I laughed.

'And how old did you say you were?'

'I didn't, but I'm twenty.'

Jesper just shook his head.

The week before my debut I went back to Arboga to see my family, but also to say hi to Wiggo. We had kept in close contact and he gave me a sense of security and confidence in my faith that I really needed. He gave me Communion at home and a final blessing, one I would repeat before all my fights. There was only one occasion when I couldn't do the blessing before the fight, or rather I didn't bother, and that turned out to be a big mistake.

In the middle of November I boarded the ferry to Finland. Travelling by boat doesn't really suit my impatient side. It felt like it took forever, and it wasn't made any better by not being allowed to drink. That's usually the best way to make the time go faster on the ferry. Mads, the coach from Stockholm Shoot who came with us, could clearly see how agitated I was. He smiled and promised I'd be able to move about properly before too long.

Eventually the boat moored up in Helsinki harbour and me,

Mads, Nico and Martin were met by one of the promoters who drove us up to Lahtis.

The event was due to start at seven o'clock, and there were seven of us Swedes on the bill. Mine was fight number five, and as usual I was absolutely nerve-stricken as I walked into the hall.

Martin had lost his fight, but Nico had taken out his opponent in the first round. I didn't want to be worse than Nico. When the ref shouted 'Fight!' a few minutes later, I sprayed kicks, punches and jabs at my opponent.

Like in my amateur fights, I didn't really think about what was going on. I heard Mads's voice as if he were a long way away. 'C'mon Alex, more! Hit him in the face, Alex!'

I did as I was told. Suddenly the bell rang for the end of the round. Five minutes had felt like five seconds.

The second round had barely got going when the ref stopped the fight. I had won but couldn't work out how. I was on all fours, gasping for air and holding my opponent. When I got up, I asked Mads what had happened. I had a complete blank and could only remember snippets of the match. I knew I had floored him at least once.

'You choked him into submission!' he said.

I was surprised, and when I watched a video of the fight it was as though I had never experienced what the replay showed me doing. In the ring I was transformed into another person. That person was separate from the normal me.

Whatever had happened, it meant my pro debut was over and naturally I felt relief. Even stronger was the desire to fight again as soon as possible.

I wouldn't have to wait too long. Barely a month later August called and said he had a pro fight for me at the Finn Fight 9 club in Turku.

The journey over the Baltic was no more fun this time than it had been the last. This time at least I didn't have to sit in a car for hours on the other side. I had slept on the boat because the event started at lunchtime and my fight was first on the bill. It was a Saturday and very cold outside. On the way to the venue I can remember freezing my arse off as I watched people stream in to watch.

My opponent was once again a Finn, Mikael Haydari, and like before I went at him like a psycho when the ref gave us the nod. Total attack, no tactics. That was my fighting style in those early days. I moved as if I was still street fighting. I chased my opponent around the ring, and when he tried to get hold of my legs I got him with a right-hander. He lost consciousness and the match was over after fifty seconds.

Again, I couldn't remember a thing. I didn't even know I'd won. As usual, it was up to the coach to tell me.

'Did he beat me?'

'Mm,' smiled the coach. 'Tough fight, that.'

As I was standing in the corner watching the other fights on the bill a short guy about my age came over and introduced himself as Manos. He congratulated me on my victory and said he had watched my pro debut, too. He had been in Lahti to take a look at my opponent.

'Afraid you didn't have much to look at,' I said.

'Well, you made short work of him. I had had great hopes for that boy . . .'

We chatted a bit more and Manos told me he had ended up becoming a manager by accident when his girlfriend's brother wanted someone to arrange MMA fights for him. In real life Manos was an electrician and arranging fixtures had become a bit of a hobby for him. He didn't make any money from it, but people kept asking him to organise the fights and he liked the sport.

'By the way, you're Swedish, I take it?'

'Of course,' I said. 'Why do you ask?'

'Because you talk like a Yugoslavian,' he said and laughed.

Maybe there was something to it. If you hang about with immigrant guys for all your teenage years, then you end up talking like them.

Manos struck me as a solid guy, but I never suspected that the little Greek luck sent me would become such an important person in my life.

Neither could I know that the next Greek to cross my path would be just as important. It was a few weeks after the win in Turku and I caught him watching me during a boxing session. When I asked the coach who he was, I was told it was Andreas Michael, coach of the Swedish national boxing team. It seemed word had got around that I fought exceptionally hard and fast for a beginner. Andreas had come down to Stockholm Shoot to see if there was any truth in it. He obviously thought so, because after the session he came up to me.

'Fancy coming to my club for a bit of sparring?'

A few days later I went along to Djurgårdens Sports Club's training gym on Norra Agnegatan. It was like climbing into a time machine back to my time at BK Köping and my early training sessions. Andreas put me in the ring with one of his guys, and when we were finished he took me aside and said he thought I was a 'natural born killer' and a 'super striker'.

Later on I found out Andreas had grown up in Greek Cyprus and the UK. He spoke great English and would mix it liberally with Swedish. It was the way we talked to each other for a long time after.

'You have the right instincts, but we have to improve your technique,' he said, and among other things told me I was going in with my head too high. It was what I had always done, my style. Anyway, I did what Andreas told me to the letter.

I did a few more sessions up on Norra Agnegatan. After that Andreas started to come to Stockholm Shoot and coach me there himself. Did he make me drop my head though? Not an inch. On the other hand, he managed to instil in me a whole range of skills and improvements.

Around then August got in touch and said he had started a company to arrange MMA fights. The first one was going to be held in Stockholm on 9 February and he had already put my name on the bill. The fights were coming thick and fast, which worked for me because I desperately needed to pick up match experience. My opponent was a guy called Farbod Fadami from Germany. I had no idea who he was, nor did I care. The only thing for me was to make sure I was prepared when the day came.

And I was prepared. When that Saturday arrived at the start of February, I had so much energy in my body that I exploded as soon as the ref gave the sign. Farbod managed to get hold of my leg, but my takedown defence had improved a lot and I floored him with his own hold.

On the mat I hit him and hit him until the ref finished the fight, two and a half minutes into the first round. Suddenly something entirely new to me happened. The whole crowd got on their feet and started shouting, 'A-lex, A-lex, A-lex!' I was still a shy guy and never felt comfortable being the centre of attention, but this was totally different. This was proof I had done something good, and I can truthfully say it gave me a genuine shiver of excitement down my spine.

That feeling would return several times in the course of 2008. A month or so later it was time for another match. This time it was a private event in the UAE. I remember how great it was flying down and feeling that heat, packing my swimming trunks and going a day early. I also remember thinking what a cool and crazy place Dubai was with all the skyscrapers and artificial lakes in the middle of the desert.

The event itself was kind of crazy, held in a conference hall with only a few hundred in the crowd. There were loads of tables ringside with white cloths where sheikhs sat about drinking and relaxing, as if the fights were just dinner entertainment for them. Me and the other guys had to parade around the ring for them. We each had a T-shirt with a number on so the sheikhs could vote by text on who they wanted to match up.

I think I was number two, and the sheikhs voted for me to take on a German – again – called Florian Muller.

As usual I went in hard, taking him down and unleashing my

fists and elbows on him. The ref had to stop halfway through the round so they could wipe the blood off his face. Then I carried on grounding and pounding him. He was a bit wimpy and waited out until time was up.

The second round was much like the first. I had him on his back and worked him, to the point where after a while the crowd got bored at the lack of competition. The ref pulled us both back to our feet, and with a minute or so left I finished him off with a knee to the body and a right-hander.

The idea was that the winners from the four matches would go on to fight a semi-final at another event. Whoever won the title could expect 75,000 dollars in prize money. The problem was that the Dutch promoter went bankrupt, so there were no more fights. Promoters failing to make the sums add up is unfortunately not uncommon. It has been true of boxing and other combat sports for years.

After Dubai I won my fifth pro fight on a technical knockout, against an Italian called Matteo Minonzio. It was an event in Gothenburg that August had organised. A few days later August told me he'd been in contact with a manager who was young and new to the game, but who seemed to be sharp.

'I reckon he could help you get a UFC contract.'

'Seriously?' I said.

'Sure, he was the one who fixed Per Eklund up with a deal.'

Per Eklund was a name everyone had heard of. He was the first Swede in the UFC and had made his debut earlier that year, only a few weeks before I won my fight in Stockholm. Annoyingly he had lost his first UFC fixture, but people at the gym hoped he would get another chance to prove himself soon.

'What, you reckon he'd be interested in me?' I wondered.

'Yep, seems so. You should meet him at any rate. His name is Manos Terzitane.'

The name rang a bell. Wasn't that what the Greek guy had been called? The one who came up to me after the Finland fight?

I recognised him straight away when we met in Stockholm a few weeks later. He had quickly built up a good roster of fighters, who came to him because they knew he took care of his boys. He'd had a bit of luck when Bosse Ringholm, the sports minister, had tried to ban MMA in Sweden. The whole business had hung in the balance and suddenly a load of fighters were drifting about without contracts. Manos came out of nowhere and soon had a monopoly, putting pressure on the promoters as soon as the government stopped threatening to close the sport down. Guys who had only been paid a few thousand kronor for fights were suddenly getting 75,000 or more. When the promoters rang and tried to get fighters on the old terms Manos was quick to answer, 'No way. We're living in different times.'

Some of the promoters got pissed off and stopped dealing with Manos or any of his roster. The public knew which fighters they wanted, though, and the guys who didn't play ball were soon out of business.

Manos wasn't all that interested by the money. He did what he did for his boys, and because he enjoyed it. Me and Manos never signed a contract, we agreed verbally what our terms were. The truth is, even now we don't have a contract that means we have to do stuff. At any rate, he was good to me and promised to arrange fights that could get me into the UFC. Because Manos had the best fighters on his roster, he also made sure I trained against top guys. One of the first people he paired me with was a multiple Swedish wrestling champion from the Rosengård project, in Malmö, called Ilir Latifi. He was also known as 'The Sledgehammer' in the ring, and he taught me a lot about being on the ground.

Things began to fall into place. I had a manager, a string of cool training buddies and an outstanding boxing coach. With Andreas and Manos by my side, I had the right people in position to start the long climb to the top.

The climb was not going to be easy. I carried on the sessions at

Stockholm Shoot and worked as a doorman at different bars and as a builder in-between. One night in the early autumn of 2008 I was watching the door of a nightclub on Södermalm in Stockholm. It was almost midnight and people were getting rowdy and playing up. I was busy trying to stop two guys who were threatening to get heavy when my mobile buzzed in my pocket.

It was Manos. As he had promised, he had been working to get me European fights. Even so I was surprised when he asked me, 'How does a fight in Poland sound?'

'Great!' I said. 'When?'

'Tomorrow.'

When the club closed, I went straight home and packed my bag. Nico was coming, too, and I shared a taxi with him to Arlanda airport to catch the first possible flight to Katowice. There we were picked up and driven to a town called Dąbrowa Górnicza, a place I had never heard of before in my life.

I fought against a Polish guy called Krzysztof Kulak with twenty-one wins in his pocket, winning it on a unanimous decision by the judges. It was the first time I'd had to go a whole three rounds, and boy I felt it. The other thing you have to remember is that if you start to flag in the ring, or in a cage with everyone watching, then the fall is monumental. It isn't like football, where you can have a bad game and come out fresh the next time. In this business, if you don't perform you are quickly yesterday's news.

It wasn't only the effort and the three rounds that meant I staggered out of the ring. I was totally sleep-deprived. I wasn't allowed to sleep then, either. An hour or so later it was time to go back to Katowice, and then back home to Stockholm.

It was those kinds of trips that made Dania more and more frustrated with me. There were also the training camps that Manos organised. Like any girl she wanted her boyfriend at home, and one day when I came home from the building site and started to pack my suitcase, she lost it.

'Jesus, all your damn training drives me mad. Do you not see that?'

I didn't see it. What I did see was a need to train as much as I was, if I wanted to move up a level. Either I gave everything, sacrificed everything, or I might as well chuck it all in and do something else instead. The thing was, there wasn't anything else for me. MMA was my life. Despite the arguments Dania was there to pep me up and support me when I felt down. Sometimes I would work nights as well as all day, doing a shift at the building site then going to work at a bar. That I fought as much as possible was also because I needed the money.

Sure, I was a pro and was fighting on the continent, but I was no star and didn't have a string of sponsors behind me. That was something I could only dream of, for it would have made everything easier. But I knew all that could be mine with as little as one fight. The 'fight or finish' mentality in MMA means that sponsors can come knocking just as quick as they can vanish if you lose. That is how it works.

One day Manos was in an unusually good mood when I met him. Per Eklund had won his second UFC fixture, the first Swede ever to do so. He also said UFC had shown an interest in me, but that it was still too early. Nobody had promised me anything concrete, but those words pushed me to another victory with a technical knockout in the first round at the start of November.

Suddenly nobody was giving me fights. Manos explained that he wanted to match me with people at the right level to showcase what I could do for UFC. It was about strategy. I kept training hard anyway and made progress in the gym. Andreas came more often and coached me at Stockholm Shoot, and you could see he was really getting into MMA.

As a junior boxer I had beaten a guy in the national championships called David Loy. He had carried on boxing and fought all over, including in Germany. He got in touch asking to fight me in a rematch, which was a bit odd when you think how much time had passed since that first one. Our coach arranged for us to meet anyway, and I looked forward to it, as it gave me a chance to really test my boxing skills. I was also still waiting for another MMA fight that never seemed to materialise, so the boxing was a way of keeping my body and thirst for competition satisfied.

At the end of February me and David fought our heavyweight rematch at a ring in Rinkeby in the Stockholm suburbs. Just like I had the last time, I won all five rounds on points. It felt nice, but it didn't do much in the long term. MMA was what I was after. Eventually I got my fix, a home fixture in Stockholm at the end of May 2009. I had now turned twenty-two and was hungry to push on. I showed it by knocking out my opponent a few minutes into the first round.

Did it make UFC get in touch? When I asked Manos, he shook his head. I asked him to set up as many fights as he could, in Sweden and abroad. I thought I might as well push on and get stuck in. Eventually they'd have to take me. Soon enough Manos had organised five fights in six months for me. It was perfect; if nothing else it meant money coming in and match practice.

A few days later Manos came to see me at the gym and looked really troubled.

'Alex, I've five bits of bad news and one good one.'

'Ah, right,' I said, fearing the worst.

'Well, the first fight we had you booked in for is cancelled. So is the second, and the third, and the fourth and fifth.'

'Why? What the hell happened?'

His frown turned into a smile.

'UFC called me. They want you.'

Chapter 8
Pro and Poor

heard people saying that this was the real test, that I hadn't yet fought anybody with talent. It was the usual Swedish shit about nobody getting above their station. People often try and kick you down when you're on your way up.

After my fight with Thiago Silva at UFC Sweden, 14 April 2012.

Fighting Shogun in Seattle, 8 December 2012.

Title fight between me and Jon Jones in Toronto, 21 September 2013.

A bit of a staredown between me and Jones before our fight. Dana White is in the background.

In a hospital in Toronto with Jones after our fight.

Me, Andreas, Manos, Majdi and Gabbe in Dubai Mall, spring 2014.

Guest fighters with Jimi Manuwa in Abu Dhabi after our fight, spring 2014.

Before the press conference in Las Vegas, autumn 2015. From left: Lyoto Machida, Chris Weidman, me, Ronda Rousey, Conor McGregor, Jon Jones and Anderson Silva.

With Jones before the press conference.

With Andreas at Outdoor World, Las Vegas.

San Diego before the fight against Anthony Johnson: Me, Jocke and Jimmy.

Celebrating my birthday in San Diego.

The summer of 2009 had started well. I had won my eighth straight pro match. I was on a list of the top ten most promising MMA fighters in Europe compiled by the website Sherdog, and best of all, I had a contract with UFC on the table.

When things were that good, feeling happy with life wasn't a challenge. Even if you don't have a lot of cash and are living in a small flat with a girl who isn't exactly overjoyed by you spending all your spare time at the gym. But what else could I do? A UFC contract was something I hadn't even dared dream about when I started at Gladius two years before, and now it was actually happening.

When the day was done and I'd ripped down a wall or painted a house or installed some windows, I would take my gym bag and go straight from the worksite to train. I would run myself into the ground, so when I got home all Dania saw was a boyfriend who could hardly open his mouth.

Sometimes I didn't even go home after training. I would head straight to a bar to watch the door until closing time. Then she didn't see me at all. It hardly helped that I worked weekends as well. It was as if I wanted it that way . . .

One Saturday night at some club, a guy I worked with came over and said the owner wanted no Poles in the club, but we should try and get in more girls off the street.

'He says the Poles are always hammered when they arrive and never buy anything inside. They come to chat up girls, but the ladies leave, as does everyone else.'

I sighed. As if keeping people off-their-face in line wasn't hard enough, I also had to work for a low-level racist. However much I would have loved to walk away, I really needed that job.

Even my manager Manos didn't have the money to do MMA full time. I was still doing his work as an electrician, even though he had built up a roster of promising fighters from across the continent. In MMA you have to reach a high level to make a living from it. Neither me or Manos were there yet. We were pros, but pros without any money.

It was a tough situation. I worked hard to improve my fighting, and worked hard at the building sites, and hard at the club doors. I would never have managed it without financial help from my family. Through a friend I managed to get the tiny flat down in Blåsut that me and Dania shared. The problem was that Dania couldn't get a job, and it didn't help I worked for her dad. Luckily Jimmy had started his own building firm in Stockholm and I could work for him instead.

If you ignore how little money we had and the constant hunt to get some, then it was all-in-all a good summer. I was wired about fighting in the UFC, and at the start of September I finally signed the contract. It was an indescribable feeling. That was it done. I was playing in the premier league, and I was going to do everything to show people that was where I belonged.

One of the first people to ring was Carlos.

'Man, you were right when you said I'd be in the UFC in a few years.'

'Of course I was,' said Carlos. 'I didn't doubt you for a second.'

About the same time August Wallén got in touch. He had heard the news about the UFC contract and made me an offer. I would get 10,000 a month and a flat in Gothenburg if I moved back and trained at Gladius. The fact I almost bit his hand off says a lot about how tired I was of struggling to support me and Dania. More than anything else, it meant I could train one hundred per cent. It was a great chance.

A week or so after I had signed the contract with UFC me and Dania moved to Gothenburg. There wasn't much to pack into the van we hired, which was lucky because the new place was even smaller than the old one. I could see the disappointment in Dania's eyes, but she didn't say anything. She had come along for my sake, with no friends in Gothenburg and nothing to do. Everything was set for a perfect storm.

When I look back on it, I can see how naïve I was in taking up August on his offer. I mean, 10,000 krona a month? I've had mates take the piss out of me for being so stupid, but back then I thought it great to not be working on building sites and on the club doors. It meant no more being exhausted or feeling I had never trained enough. Now I was free to do it, and that was all that mattered. In a few months I would have my first UFC fight, and nothing could distract me from it.

I heard people saying that this was the real test, that I hadn't fought anybody with talent. It was the usual Swedish shit about nobody getting above their station. People often try and kick you down when you're on your way up. It is all part of the game, and to be honest I didn't think too much about it, but concentrated on getting into shape and improving my technique.

At Gladius August was my main coach again. He was also the one who gave me my fighting name, 'The Mauler'. He thought it was better than 'The Outlaw', the name my training buddy Reza 'Mad Dog' Madadi had given me. I couldn't help but agree.

In the run-up to the fight the deal between me and August worked well enough. I guess I really didn't care too much about a lot of stuff then, because I was living on the kick I got from the UFC contract. It was also great to be able to train as much as I wanted. Perhaps Dania had been hoping to see more of me now I wasn't chasing different jobs, but all my time freed up from not working went straight into training. There was no change as far as she was concerned. She was as lonely as before. I couldn't help but notice how bad she was feeling from sitting in that tiny flat with nothing to do. At the same time, I was so focused on making my first UFC fight a victory that I couldn't do anything to help her.

It is tough to describe what the mood was like at the hotel where all the fighters stayed in Manchester. You could feel the nervousness hanging in the air. Me, August and Nico got there a few hours before the weigh-in and didn't think too much about it, but breakfast on the day of the fight was horrible. It was like everyone had their guard up. Plates and cutlery rattled and ended up on the floor. I couldn't even bring myself to eat. Even at lunch I had no appetite, and when it was time to get on the UFC bus to the arena I was sick with anxiety, alternating between sweating and shivering.

In the changing room there was an even more nervous wait. I must have gone to the toilet a hundred times for a piss, and when they bandaged my hands I could hardly sit still.

Because I hadn't eaten, I had taken a banana with me from the hotel, thinking I would eat it before the fight. The problem was the doping tests done by UFC were strict. You weren't allowed water or food in the changing room, so I had to wolf it down in the corridor under the watchful eye of a match official.

My fight was second on the bill, so I didn't have to wait long, which was good. Not only because I am naturally restless, but because I avoided having to sit and listen to the sound of the other fights. When you're sat in the changing room you can hear every smack and roar of the crowd and how the fighters go down, one after the other.

All I had to do was wait for the first fight to finish, then I took a deep breath and got ready for my walkout.

UFC events are always bigger and more professionally done. The biggest difference is the crowd, because when you walk out to a crowd that big, it is one huge rumble. That's when you know there is no way back. It's now or never.

I thought about tactics, playing the fight out in my head. Well, I did until I got inside the cage. After that I didn't think at all. My mouth was dry. I could feel my heartbeat in my temples and I was so full of adrenalin that if anyone had asked me a question I would have lamped them. You spend so much time building up and are only ready to do one thing. As my opponent Jared Hamman climbed into the Octagon I could make out August's voice above the roar.

'Come on, Alex! This is everything we've worked so hard for!'

A second later the ref shouted, 'Fight!' Weirdly, I didn't go blank this time. I was totally focused on reading my opponent to try and find a weakness, which I did. After forty seconds I planted a right-hander on his cheek. He landed on his back without breaking his fall. I spat out my gumshield I was so eager and went over to finish him. I hardly had time to land another blow before the ref stopped the fight. I was euphoric.

That Christmas was the first time in a while that I could hang out with the people closest to me in Arboga. It had been a long time coming, because everything had happened at once. But soon after New Year, it was time to get back into the gym again. UFC were happy with my performance and had arranged another fight for me, this time against Phil Davis from the US, in Abu Dhabi that April. Phil was a good wrestler, so I needed to work on that part of my play. Put another way, I needed to get better at everything if I was to carry on to the top.

That was when the problems started. After a week or so at the training camp at Gladius I felt it wasn't working – I didn't have the opposition I needed. The sparring partners August gave me weren't good enough. Sometimes he would send a guy weighing 70 kilos to fight me. It was a complete joke. When you're fighting UFC you can't train against people on a lower level. You have to constantly try and find sparring partners who are at least as good as you are, and ideally a bit better. It was as if August hadn't grasped that.

It was also clear that Gladius didn't have the experience of fighting at the level I had reached. Sure, they had a professional squad, but there's a big gap between being a pro and fighting in the UFC. On top of that, August still had his own ideas about *how* I should train. Whenever I suggested testing new techniques he always shook his head. Maybe we could have sorted it out if we had talked to each other, but it simply didn't work. He thought his way was the only way, and wasn't even prepared to meet me in the middle.

The only one who could give me what I needed was Andreas, but he was still busy with the national boxing squad and could only make it down to Gothenburg every so often. It wasn't an optimal situation, and I began to lose both my confidence and my motivation. MMA is about emotional strength and good mental health more than people might think. You can be as athletic as you like, but if you're not happy about yourself or don't have the belief, then chances are you're heading for defeat.

That late winter of 2010 I suffered. It was a hopeless uphill struggle against the poor quality of training and my own lack of motivation. I did what I could to hide my feelings and I managed to fool everyone but Andreas.

'What's the matter with you?' he asked, during a break in our final boxing session before my next fight. 'You're going to Abu Dhabi in a few days for another UFC fight. Most guys can only dream of this stuff, but you look like a dead man. You're not there. What is it?'

He looked me in the eye, but I avoided his gaze and said, 'Ah, nothing.'

What could I tell him? That I felt like shit and wanted him to come to Abu Dhabi with me instead of going to Turkey with the boxing squad?

I could see he didn't buy it. The problem was, back then we didn't know each other well enough for him to put me on the spot. He shook his head and we carried on with the session.

The boxing tour of Turkey was important to Andreas, too. He wanted to become the top coach in the world and was hoping to lead out his country at the 2012 Olympics in London. That my fight against Phil Davis was the same day as the final of the Turkey tournament was just bad luck.

I don't want to make excuses for myself. There could be no blame game. Fact was, though, there was a lot wrong in the build-up to my meeting with Phil. It wasn't only the training, my lack of motivation and Andreas not being there. For whatever reason, I never made it to Arboga to get my blessing from Wiggo. I think I told myself I didn't have time, but the truth was that deep down I did not want to do that fight. I was totally unbalanced.

Until then I had always felt wired before fights, but when I got on the plane to Abu Dhabi I was anything but. It was a weird and uncomfortable feeling to be on the way to an event I should have been excited about but felt like ducking out of. By the time we got to the hotel on Yas Island in Abu Dhabi I was pretty ambivalent. I'm not a natural showman, in fact I am terrible at pretending. Now I had to, both at the weigh-in and during the international press conferences. I told them all I couldn't wait and was sure I'd chalk up my second UFC win.

On the day of the fight, me and the team got to the arena in good time. Back in Sweden it was early spring and there was a chill in the air, but there it was burning hot and there was sand everywhere. Well, everywhere except the unbelievably green strips alongside the six-lane motorway. Through the car widow I saw immigrant workers in overalls and sun hats struggling to pull out weeds and clip bushes. I can't understand how they didn't die from the heat.

For the first time ever, at least I didn't feel nervous. As I warmed up in the changing room, Nico patted me on the shoulder and said, 'Wake the hell up, man! You're not yourself today!'

I really wasn't and this was not my day.

When I climbed into the Octagon it was like I was at the side watching myself. I had more or less screwed it up before the ref even started the fight.

Despite that, the first round against Phil was good enough, or it was for the first few minutes at least. We had a minute or so left and I tried to take him down, but ended up on the floor myself and in the grip of an anaconda choke. It happened so fast I didn't have time to react. It was either tap out or pass out. Five measly seconds of the first round were left when I smacked my hand on the floor. Later on I would hear people say I had given up too early, that I should have held out for those last few seconds. I didn't have a fighter's heart, they said. I wanted to tell them to go and see how it feels to be strangled. You get tired of it really quick.

After the match I felt empty inside. I congratulated Phil and his coach, and made some joke about getting them to train me up on my wrestling. Phil took me at face value and said I was welcome at his gym in San Diego whenever I wanted. It is typical of how the sport works actually. Fighters take care of each other and try to help each other out if they can. But right then I couldn't honestly contemplate any training, or any more fights. I was a beaten man, and I felt no better when I got back to Gothenburg a day later.

I rang Carlos, who did all he could to cheer me up.

'Everyone loses a fight eventually. It's no big deal. The important thing is that you go on from this and build on it. Look at it as a lesson. You lost the fight because you didn't do what you should have. You still have the talent. You need to complement it with all your time, all your spirit, and all your will.'

Carlos didn't stop there.

'Losing can be a good thing, because it teaches you so much. To take a setback and turn it into something positive is what separates a real champion from the other fighters.'

He was right, but I felt too bad to take any of it onboard, and a few days later I felt Gothenburg was no longer an option for me. Simply being at Gladius gave me episodes of panic, and I rang Andreas.

'Andreas, I am moving to Stockholm. I can't stay here!'

Andreas sounded a little surprised, but he said, 'OK, speak with August first so you don't run off without telling anyone.'

I did as he asked and rang August, who was in Thailand for the Thai Boxing World Championships. August asked me to wait until he was back in Sweden before making a decision. The thing was, as soon as I put the phone down I knew I couldn't. I dialled Jimmy's number.

'I need help. I need to move now.'

'OK,' said Jimmy calmly. 'You mean you want out straight away?'

'Yeah, NOW!'

It was Thursday, and that same evening Jimmy came down from Stockholm with a van he had got hold of. We loaded everything that me and Dania owned, which is to say what little we had in the flat. For her part, Dania seemed relieved to be leaving Gothenburg behind as well.

'Are you sure you don't want to wait a few hours so we can tell the guys at the gym?' asked Jimmy, for what seemed like the hundredth time, as we all sat rammed into the van. It was the middle of the night and the street lay empty in front of us.

I shook my head.

'No, just drive.'

So we drove out of Gothenburg, away from Gladius and towards the dawn and Dania's parents' house in Arboga. We dropped her off. Our relationship had not been good for a long time, but we hadn't put the final nail in the coffin. This was the end, though.

Me and Jimmy drove on to Mum and Kalle's place in Boda and got rid of most of the stuff there. Then we went to see Grandma, who made us breakfast and asked us to rest for a few hours before going on. We hadn't slept a wink the entire night. All I wanted was to get to Stockholm as soon as possible, and to get back my life there.

Chapter 9
Alliance

I f you want to carry on with MMA then you need to live for it. You have to throw your heart and soul into it. Otherwise it won't work.

'So, here I am!'

After a few hours of sleep at Jimmy's place, I had driven straight over to Andreas. He looked at me with a hint of surprise through the gap in the door.

'That was quick. Have you spoken to anyone at Gladius?'

'I called August, and he wanted me to wait till he was back.'

'But you didn't?'

I shook my head.

'I couldn't do it.'

Real friends are there for each other when you really need it. Andreas did just that. He welcomed me in and asked what I wanted to do. I said I was thinking about stopping fighting and working as a carpenter or something in the building trade. I may have had no education to speak of, but at least I knew my way around a building site. Andreas thought I should carry on training at the very least, and I guess that was what I had come over to hear him say. Why else had I gone looking for him?

I still didn't really know what I wanted. The defeat against Phil had really broken me. It wasn't that I hated losing – he had made me feel like an amateur, and that feeling was the one I hated most of all.

Andreas promised to help me as much as I needed if I really did decide to carry on fighting. He told me that he felt bad about not being there in Abu Dhabi. It was almost like he wanted to take the blame for me losing. He also told me he had realised where his heart really was: not in boxing but in MMA.

Speaking to him felt good. The thing was, in the same way he felt bad about me losing, I soon had cause to feel sorry for him. August and the others back at Gladius were convinced that Andreas was behind my leaving and accused him of stealing me.

So much shit was said that eventually Andreas had to have a crisis meeting with August.

Whilst all this was going on I went back to working as a doorman, and soon got back the bug to go and train. There was this energy all through my body. It was mostly about revenge, or I guess you could say I wanted to prove to myself that I had much more to give than what the crowd had seen that night in Abu Dhabi.

When I got to Stockholm Shoot, however, it didn't quite work. My body wanted to get going, but nothing else did. I wasn't there. It is a horrible feeling when nothing works, it hangs over you and I can imagine it is similar for a lot of other athletes. Suddenly a tennis star starts missing all their first serves and makes fault after fault. Or a golf pro loses their swing and the balls end up in bunkers and ponds. It has nothing to do with physical condition, which makes it even harder to deal with.

When the session was over, I sat in the changing room for ages and stared at the wall.

After a while Tommy and Antonio came in and found me. Antonio had moved into Jimmy's place in the flats in Rågsved with me, and even though I felt like shit it was still great to be living with two of my oldest mates.

'I'm gonna stop,' I said before either of them had time to speak.

'Ah, you don't mean that,' said Jimmy. He sat down beside me on the bench.

'Of course I do,' I replied. I fell apart as I said it. I think I was mostly angry, but instead of getting out my aggression by smacking or kicking something, I leaned forward with my face in my hands and started to cry.

'Alex, look at yourself,' said Jimmy. 'You've got something good here and God only knows where it might take you. If you really fight for this you could be the best in the world. Give up now and you'll only ever have got halfway. Is that what you really want?'

I didn't answer but looked up at him with red eyes.

'No, didn't think so. Sharpen up, man.' He put his hand on my shoulder. 'Come on, let's go sink a few pints and find some fun.'

'Yeah, c'mon Alex,' said Antonio. 'We can go into town. The weather's beautiful.'

There was no point sitting there being difficult, so I went with them. Antonio was right – it really was a great evening. Stockholm looked like a travel brochure when we came out of the metro at Slussen station and looked over the water. Suddenly I noticed how fit the girls were, too, and remembered that I was single.

I'm a relationship kind of guy. I've always had girlfriends and don't like being alone. It was inevitable I'd meet someone else fairly soon after me and Dania finished with each other. Her name was Sikina and that night was our first encounter.

My mood can turn from black to bright sunshine on a sixpence. Whichever way my mood turns, it happens quick. That's how I am, and a couple of days after I felt like I wanted to give up on MMA, I suddenly found I wanted to get back in the gym.

As I said, in MMA you always compete with a fight-or-finish mentality. I'd had two fights, winning one and losing the other. That meant I had one final chance to prove I belonged at that level. Manos had told me that UFC would give me another fight, but if I didn't perform then the contract would be torn up. All the same, I felt motivated and happy, perhaps because I was back at Stockholm Shoot. It also felt good to be coached by Andreas again. Of course, there were days when the training didn't quite work out, and I was still in a bad situation with money. The idea of going back to full-time work was quite attractive.

Being poor is something you have to experience yourself if you want to know how tough it feels. Sometimes I didn't have enough to eat, but when that happened whoever had cash in the gang would fork out for a meal for the rest of us. That was how it worked. We helped each other to survive. Even Andreas did it in those early UFC days – either he would buy me food or I'd end up doing the same for him.

In the middle of the summer I finally had news of another fight for me. I was going to fight a Frenchman called Cyrille Diabaté in a UFC event at the O2 Arena in London on 16 October. Cyrille was unbeaten in almost three years and I was the underdog. The disappointment I suffered after my loss was long gone, but sometimes I still felt I was underperforming in the gym. It was on one such day that Andreas told me, 'If you want to carry on with MMA then you need to live for it. You have to throw your heart and soul into it. Otherwise it won't work.'

It made me think about what I had said to Phil Davis and his coach after the fight in Abu Dhabi. Half-jokingly I had remarked that I should train with them to improve my wrestling technique, and they had said I was welcome to go over to the gym in San Diego. I told Andreas, who looked thoughtful for a moment.

'That's not a bad idea,' he said. 'It would be fuckin' great if you could spar against Phil and get him to teach you to wrestle.'

'You're my coach. Tell me what you think we should do,' I said.

The day before, Andreas had mentioned a training camp at a gym in London he knew. The idea was that London would give me access to better opposition, but now he called California. Training against the person who had beaten me was the best thing I could hope for, because it would purge the defeat from my mind. The risk was that if I didn't get over it, then it would plague me forever.

A while later Andreas came back and gave me a thumbs-up sign.

'I spoke to Phil's coach, Eric Del Fierro. He says all we have to do is get on a plane.'

The news really perked me up. It was like someone had handed my life back to me.

'Great,' I said. 'We can try some new stuff. Things can only get better from here.'

A few weeks later me and Andreas flew to London to take part in training sessions at London Shootfighters. We were allowed to stay for free at a house that belonged to the gym owners. It was real budget stuff. Andreas called us the 'Road Warriors'.

London was sweaty, and when we flew home to Stockholm it felt nice to get away from that close heat. But we didn't stay in

Sweden for long. At the end of August we made the big step across the Atlantic. It was a step that I felt in every inch of my body.

Me and Andreas were both exhausted with jet-lag when, after a lot of chopping and changing, we jumped into a taxi in San Diego to go to Chula Vista, the place that Alliance MMA called home in a big single-storey building.

We got a friendly welcome from both the staff and from Phil's coach Eric. When he found out how little money we had, he said straight away that we could sleep at the gym until we found somewhere we could afford. We thanked him, threw down our bags and went out to find some cheap food. We soon grasped how much that part of California was influenced by its closeness to Mexico. There were loads of great little restaurants with Mexican food for pennies. Compared to London it was a dream.

After eating we fell into a food coma pretty quick. When we got back to the gym we hardly had time to undress before we both collapsed onto the mattresses we had been given. I slept like a log, but was woken up by a banging sound a few hours later. It took a minute for me to work out what it was, and when I checked my watch I saw it wasn't even seven a.m. yet.

I pulled on my jeans and went into the gym. Phil Davis was in there on his own, going hard at a punch-bag. I rubbed my eyes, involuntarily impressed by his discipline, and went over to say hi.

He smiled when he saw me and we chatted a little. It was weird to be standing there on the other side of the world, wide awake thanks to the time difference, shaking hands with a guy who only months before had been choking me in front of a crowd of sheikhs. It was no less weird that this guy was going to help me get good enough that I might even take him down in a revenge match.

Andreas came in and said hi to Phil too, then turned to me and smiled knowingly.

'Why don't you get up to train at seven in the morning like this guy?'

He knew exactly which buttons to push. Next morning the alarm was set for five forty-five a.m. By six I was changed and going hard at the punch-bag. Andreas stumbled half-asleep into the otherwise empty gym and just stared at me. An hour later, Phil arrived. I was completely covered in sweat. Phil gave me a broad smile.

The ice had been broken and I was soon part of the gang at Alliance. I wasn't as chatty as some of the other boys, but the sparring was good, irrespective of whether it was Phil or another top fighter pushing my limits at grappling and wrestling.

We did at least two sessions a day, six days a week. They went on until they bled. Those guys had a totally different attitude to the sport than most of us Swedes. It wasn't a hobby for them, more like a matter of life and death. They had this intense drive. After a week at Alliance I hadn't only found my motivation and self-belief again, but for the first time in my life I decided what it was I wanted. I was going to put everything into MMA. I was going all in, and I would become the best in the world.

Eric Del Fierro seemed to understand what I had gone through, because he told me he'd noticed how fit I was as soon as I arrived. What was missing was the mental strength. Phil said with a smile that he was glad he'd fought me in April and not then. It was a great compliment to receive. I wanted to be as good as he was – or even better – and when I was at Alliance I watched him like a hawk. Not only his training, but what he ate and what kind of guy he was. Phil was an example to me both as a fighter and a person, and all I wanted to do was to be able to beat him.

Before the London fight we finished training in Stockholm and I arrived not only in better shape than ever, but with a changed attitude towards what lay in front of me. In Sweden we're used to always having a safety net. If we fall, society catches us. For Americans it is different; for them life is always on a knife edge. That was the feeling I wanted for myself.

It could come in useful when you were up against a four-time world Thai Boxing champion. Sure, Cyrille Diabaté was fourteen years older than I was, but that meant he was experienced rather than past it. His nickname was 'The Snake', given to him because he could strike so quick. Being the underdog again didn't bother me. UFC ranking and the odds the bookmakers give you is not important once you climb into the cage. In MMA anything can happen. One lucky punch can be enough to bring down a king, to make a favourite into a loser.

When I walked into a packed O2 Arena that October night there was no doubt in me at all. I was there to make my UFC contract concrete. And that was what I did. From the first moment I dominated the fight. I made sure Cyrille couldn't come at me with his high kicks, and showed no respect or mercy. I sent him tumbling with a punch after less than a minute.

On the floor I checked him again and again. In the second round I had him in the mount position and unleashed blow after blow at his head. I knew it was there for the taking. I finished him with a choke.

Joe Rogan did an interview with me after the win and congratulated me on controlling the fight the way I had. I was given the chance to say a few words and took the time to say thanks to everyone at Alliance. Without their help God knows how it would have ended.

I was back in the game, and it felt as if nothing could stop me. But I hadn't reckoned with the skeletons from your past that can pop up again and fuck everything up if they want.

Chapter 10
Down Under

e're not gonna let you go in the UFC with a unibrow, bro! . . . That might be the thing in Sweden, but here in California, it's no bueno, dude.

'How about it Alex?' said Jimmy, when I got back to the flat in Rågsved. 'Why don't we get all the guys together back home and celebrate the win properly?'

I was twenty-three and had just won the most important fight of my career to date. There was no question about it. We would celebrate until none of us could stand. And it had to be done 'back home' in Arboga, with everyone we knew. Anything else was not an option.

'Absolutely,' I said. 'You gonna organise it?'

''Course, Ove,' Jimmy said, jokingly using a name he had stopped calling me since we had both begun to have better luck.

It was the middle of October, and the guys worked out they could combine my victory party with Halloween. The idea was good, the result not so much.

Jimmy and Antonio got hold of a venue through the council and agreed with our mate Wilson that he would play DJ and haul everything over there. Then a few others were assigned a trip to Germany to buy a shedload of cheap spirits. And when I say a shedload, I mean it absolutely literally.

I was busy myself with getting down to training and discussing my future with Manos and Andreas. My last victory meant things were serious in a way they had never been before, even if we weren't drowning in money. I had got a bit of cash for the win and my sponsors, but everything I earned went straight back into paying for us to train and travel.

At any rate, I was due at my party back in Arboga. Because it was Halloween everyone had to be dressed up, according to Jimmy and Antonio. People looked crazy when they arrived at the venue in town. There were loads of them, and the mood was great. I went round saying hi to all the old faces, or at least the ones I recognised behind the skull masks and all the other horror costumes. I had dressed up as a kind of Mexican farmer-cum-bandit in a garish poncho and sombrero. Don't ask me why.

The spirits from Germany seemed to work like rocket fuel on most people, and the music Wilson was pumping out from his improvised DJ booth didn't exactly bring us down. We danced like maniacs and screamed our heads off. Antonio and Jimmy had properly pimped the place. I was enjoying myself, and I didn't mind all the slaps on the back I was getting either.

A lot of the guys there were not long out of prison or homes. Maybe that should have set the alarm bells ringing. The same went for the gang of Stockholm lads who walked into the room with an invite from someone in Arboga. Anyway, I was there to have fun, and that was probably why I didn't notice what was afoot. I don't think anyone did actually. By this time we were all so hammered that our powers of observation were hardly stellar.

Party bosses Jimmy and Antonio had organised some really mad games, and there was a lot of joking and laughing. It was quite simply a great party. Problem was, because I get so restless, before long I wanted to move on somewhere else to check out what was happening around town. I told the boys and said I'd be back soon.

It was Jimmy who told me what happened when I was gone. Apparently the Stockholm guys had started trying it on with some of the girls and then turned nasty. Jimmy told them where to get off, but it didn't help. Then he asked them politely but firmly to leave.

They left the building but instead started giving shit to the people standing outside, among them Antonio's nephew. Jimmy had enough and told them to fuck off. One of the guys pulled out a knife and went at Jimmy. Soon after that the whole place was chaos.

When I got back I was met with a completely insane picture. On the ground outside was a guy showing no signs of life. People were crying and screaming, and I had no idea what was going on. I was about to ask when someone called out that the police were on their way. That really stressed me out – I wanted to get the hell out of there, but I needed to find out what had happened. I found two of my mates, who told me Jimmy had been attacked. That didn't exactly calm me down and I went looking for him. Nobody, not even Antonio, knew where he was. Suddenly I heard police sirens a little way off and I realised it was time to go.

Only the day after did I finally get hold of Jimmy.

'Thank Jesus I wasn't there,' I said into my mobile. 'If I had been, I would probably have got life.'

A few weeks later Jimmy told me he had to get out of the country for a bit. He couldn't take it any more and couldn't risk ending up in those sorts of situations. Enough was enough, he thought.

'But where will you go?' I asked him.

'Singapore. I know a guy there and there's a college I could study at. Maybe I can get a job there.'

Singapore sounded a long way away. Even so, Jimmy was very much into the idea, and one day he told me it was a done deal. With that he went off to the other side of the world. I was actually impressed when he did it. My fighting career meant I had taken a similar step, now all I had to do was make sure it carried on taking me places, and away from the past I had been so close to colliding with again that October night in Arboga.

Because Jimmy was in Singapore, we had a spare place in the flat in Rågsved. My mate Perra from Köping jumped at the chance when he heard it was free. We had got to know each other through Wiggo Carlsson, who had started a discussion circle called 'young believers' that we were both part of. Just like me, Perra had a complicated background, and also like me, Wiggo was a guiding hand in his life. Now Perra had decided to follow Wiggo's teaching seriously and wanted to become a pastor himself. He was going to start at a Bible school in Stockholm, which was great because it meant he could live with me and Antonio. There was one problem: Perra wasn't the most reliable of people and needed someone to keep an eye on him. It ended up being me, even though he was the older one.

So it was that alongside putting food in my mouth and training until I collapsed, I also had to make sure Perra made it out of bed and off to Bible school every morning. It was like living with a teenager. I admit that sometimes I was no better myself. Once when Perra was asleep on the sofa I couldn't resist getting out my air gun and shooting him in the leg. He woke up with a start and squealed like a pig. Then I fired one at his arm. 'Ouch!' he bawled, looking around the room panicked but wide awake.

I couldn't keep it together and started laughing from my hiding place behind the kitchen door. Perra jumped up from the sofa and looked like he was about to kill me.

'Sorry, couldn't resist!' I shouted and made to run off.

Perra came after me at top speed, grabbed a big knife from the kitchen and hunted me around the flat. I slammed doors in his face and couldn't stop laughing.

Apart from then I was the responsible one, so when I got a call one day from one of Perra's teachers at the Bible school it was my turn to lose it. The teacher wanted to know where Perra was.

'But isn't he in class?' I said with surprise. 'I put him on the metro myself this morning.'

'Afraid not,' said the teacher. 'In fact, he hasn't been here for three weeks.'

I rang Perra and gave him an earful down the phone:

'Perra, you dickhead, you've been lying to me! You haven't been in class! Get over here right now!'

When he got back to the flat he had no choice but to come clean. Instead of going to Bible school each morning he had shuffled off to the local pizzeria in the shopping centre in Rågsved and gone to sleep on the sofa in their office. Because Perra was such a loyal customer, he and the owners had ended up becoming mates.

When I was not keeping an eye on Perra, I spent all my time training at the gym. Doing it full time was a real luxury, even if it was unbelievably hard going sometimes. Occasionally my body would not want to play ball and my coaches had to whip me. Me and Andreas in particular had our clashes – as coach he drove me hard and it was exactly what I needed, even if I did sometimes throw my gloves to the floor and storm out in a rage.

That was particularly the case when nothing seemed to be working. The frustration always subsided in the end and I would come back, smile at Andreas as he shook his head, and start again. Our relationship had got stronger and we were increasingly important to each other. I felt that with him as my coach we could go all the way. He had started to wind down his boxing activities, and one day Manos came into the gym and said UFC had a fight for me 'down under'.

'Where down under?' I asked.

'Sydney.'

My opponent was a New Zealander by the name of James Te Huna. He had only fought once at UFC level and won on a technical knockout. Impressively, he'd had his arm broken in the second round and carried on regardless. Even so, I wasn't at all scared about taking him on. He was just a career barrier to be broken.

I'd never really travelled much, but it became the norm. Because San Diego had been such good preparation for my last fight, we decided we would do part of our training camp there.

It was like meeting old friends when me and Andreas walked through the door at Alliance. Someone I was particularly happy to see again was Dominick Cruz, the first bantamweight UFC champion and a part of the training squad. He was a fun and quick-witted guy who complained I was smashing up all the fighters they had. He also said I should get a haircut, even offering to pay for it and getting the barber to do my eyebrows at the same time.

'We're not gonna let you go in the UFC with a unibrow, bro!' he said, shaking his head. 'That might be the thing in Sweden, but here in California, it's no bueno, dude.'

He was joking, but only partly. Appearance is important to a lot of fighters and apparently I hadn't been taking good enough care of either my hair or my eyebrows.

Another cool character and training buddy was Brandon Vera, and one afternoon when he and I had just finished beating each other to exhaustion, Manos rang my phone. He told me I had finally got a real sponsor, the martial arts clothing company Bad Boy.

Those January weeks in San Diego passed quickly. That isn't how camps usually feel, in fact generally it feels like you are down a mine pushing coal trucks whilst the foreman whips you. It is tough, it hurts, and it never seems to end. Alliance was different, and before I knew it, it was time to fly all the way over the Pacific from California to Sydney, where Manos was meeting us. Before me and Andreas had left for San Diego we had gone to Manos's wedding, which really was something special, even though I couldn't touch a drop of alcohol.

You might think Manos should have gone on honeymoon instead of disappearing off to Australia with me and Andreas. His wife definitely thought so, but Manos regarded my fight as too important and like so many guys before and since, had put his work first. In this case, work was also his favourite pastime, but sadly there are few women who will accept that. Manos's wife wasn't one of them, and from the start the way he prioritised his life maddened her. After a while she gave up and told him to do as he liked. After that, it wasn't long before the divorce.

When we met in Sydney, though, Manos was still a happily married man. We chatted about what we would get up to in Australia, apart from winning the fight. I knew I wanted to go diving and drive a beach buggy, and deep-sea fishing was also on the to-do list.

One day, in the run-up to the UFC event, me and the lads went on a fishing trip. I was after a real monster of a fish, or a couple of red snappers at least.

The sun shone, the sky was blue and the water was calm. Me

and Andreas sat at the stern with our rods, but Manos was less interested in catching anything and spread himself out on the deck to sunbathe. Because me and Andreas were busy trying to catch swordfish, or whatever it was we had fantasised about, we didn't pay him much attention. The fresh air and the rocking of the boat also meant we started to doze where we sat. When we woke up we realised several hours must have passed since we had last saw Manos. We got up to look for him and found him snoring on deck in his underwear, with alarmingly red skin.

'Shit, I'm fucking fried,' he groaned, when we woke him up.

That was the understatement of the trip. He was such a bright red it was almost dazzling. When we got back to the harbour and he tried to put on his shirt, he screamed in pain. All the way back to the hotel he moaned, 'Ow, ow, ouch, ow!' and said his shirt felt like sandpaper.

When we went out that night people turned and stared. A guy in a big group pointed at him and shouted, 'Look at that crazy British guy!' Later that same evening Manos started shivering and had to go back to the hotel to rest. But I still had a fight to think about, a fight that would turn out to be pretty interesting. When I walked into the arena, there was no doubt about which of us the crowd were behind. I had to hope the ref was more neutral.

To give a quick summary of the match, Te Huna took me down but couldn't do much after that. I got him in a half guard and had one of his legs pinned tight. Then I put him in a full guard, and with thirty seconds of the first round left I managed to get a choke on him after a few attempts. I'll never forget that moment. The arena went deathly quiet. Only a few seconds earlier the crowd had been so excited I couldn't hear what Andreas was calling to me, but right then you could hear a pin drop. I can honestly say I didn't care about the response; it was another step on the ladder, and one that meant I was ranked in the global top thirty for my weight class.

Soon after we got back to Sweden, sponsors started to get in touch. The first people to sound out Manos were the gambling company Unibet, who asked for a meeting. A few days later we met their CEO, Claes Bergström. We clicked immediately.

Back in those days there weren't too many outside of the small world of MMA who knew who I was. None of the big papers ever wrote about MMA and there was nothing on TV. The few times the sport ever got mentioned, it was always a story about the violence of it or supposed criminal links. Claes was of the opinion that MMA would go mainstream fairly soon, and so he was after a Swedish fighter. Sadly not everyone at Unibet was as enthusiastic as Claes, and some people opposed the deal, full stop. The good news was that Claes didn't back down and by spring 2011 we were in a position to sign a contract.

This was my second such deal, and like Bad Boy, Unibet would be one of my main sponsors in the years that followed. This was mostly down to the good working relationship we had, and I was impressed by Claes's courage in choosing to put his faith in me. Soon enough he would see the dividends of his investment – a year later MMA would make a big breakthrough in Sweden, and I was centre stage.

Chapter 11
The Mauler versus The Hammer

ndreas had organised sparring partners suited to the coming fight. Stockholm Shoot was crawling with Matyushenko clones for those few weeks, all of them trying to beat the shit out of me.

After my defeat to Phil Davis, I had pulled myself to my feet and won two fights on the bounce. What I really hoped for was to be able to take on a highly-ranked fighter. It would be great motivation, but would also mean I could climb up the rankings myself. Me and Andreas both felt I was ready to have a go at one of the sport's star names.

I had a new lease of life and you could see it in training. Things weren't dampened when Manos got in touch to say that UFC had booked me for an event in Philadelphia on 6 August. My opponent was the Belarussian Vladimir Matyushenko. He had taken the light heavyweight title in the rival International Fight League, and before that had been part of the UFC and beaten the legendary Antonio 'Little Nog' Nogueira. In other words, Matyushenko was the test I had been looking for.

One of the first things you do when you are given a fight is analyse your opponent with your coach. You look at his strengths and weaknesses and develop a game plan. Then you design your pre-fight training. A lot of MMA is about strategy, and ever since I started in the sport I have always drawn parallels with chess. Your opponent makes a move, then you make one, and you always have to be a few steps ahead.

Matyushenko was a good wrestler, so once again that was where we needed to focus.

I had also become single again, a result of the same old complaints about my training schedule taking up too much of my time. How could I put a relationship before the thing I was made for? It is who I am.

At the end of April me and some of my mates went to an MMA event at the Hovet arena in Stockholm. 'Superior Challenge 7: Rise of Champions', it was called. I was a VIP and so we got to hang about in the executive lounge with the sponsors, and in the same room was this really nice girl called Anna. There was something about her I liked and we chatted and added each other on Facebook.

When I got back to the flat in Rågsved after training the next day, I wrote her a message and asked if she wanted to go out for dinner with me.

A few hours later I got an answer: *What? You want to take me out for dinner!*

Apparently she saw me as some kind of big star, which felt a bit weird. I wrote back that I really wanted to meet her and asked if she was up for it. She was, but she lived far away in Örebro.

I went into Perra's room and gave him a shake.

'Perra, wake up!'

'What is it? What's happened?' he said.

'That girl from yesterday, you know the one, she wants to see me. Problem is she lives in Örebro.'

Perra looked at the time on his phone. It was two in the morning.

'We'll get in the car and drive over there to pick her up. Write that back.'

'No, mate, no we won't,' I said. 'It's too late and I've got to train tomorrow.' Even so, I was tempted to do what Perra had suggested and wrote back to Anna.

Got my brother here trying to persuade me to drive to Örebro and get you right now.

She answered: *If you make it let me know, and we can meet.*

It was the middle of the night and I had training in a few hours, but I really wanted to go. I took a deep breath, thought about it, and then sensibly put the idea on ice.

At the gym next day, me and Anna messaged back and forth. We wrote so many messages to each other that Andreas got pissed off and asked if I was there to practise or to mess about with my phone.

'It's a girl, boss,' I told him. He just shook his head.

When I got back to the flat that night, Perra asked how things were going with the lady in Örebro.

'Been messaging all day,' I said.

'Then what are you waiting for?' said Perra. 'Let's go!'

'Seriously?'

'Yeah, c'mon!'

When we were near Örebro, I called Anna, who said she would come and meet us at the main square in town. I don't know why, but I saw her straight away and suddenly felt really nervous.

I got out of the car and we stood there chatting. I asked if she wanted to come back to Stockholm with us. She said she did, even though she only had a tiny bag. From that evening on she lived at our place and slept in my room. It felt totally natural for some reason.

I would train all day at Stockholm Shoot and Anna hung about with Perra. I had told him to look after her, and he took his job so seriously he went along as her style adviser when she went shopping in town. After a week or so, she went back to Örebro to pick up a few things. When she got back, I felt that I had already started to miss her. There was no doubt – we were a couple.

Perra liked to think he was the matchmaker behind it all. For his hard work he was deprived of his room at the flat. It would have been a bit tight with four people, but Perra would have gone anyway, even without Anna. Wiggo was ill and Perra felt bound to take care of him, so he moved back to Köping. Then Antonio moved out, too. Soon it was just me and Anna.

Everything with Anna felt right. She came from the same neck of the woods as I did and we spoke the same language. Often we would not even need to talk, we understood each other. She also took me as I was and didn't moan about my training. There was only one problem: her ex.

Ex-boyfriends are not something I usually give much thought to, but this guy was different. He was in prison when me and Anna met and was in some kind of gang. Those kinds of guys are not normal.

'We're little fish compared to those boys,' said Perra, when I asked him about it. 'But I'll be there for you if you need it,' he added.

Soon enough this boy started sending threatening texts to Anna. Because they came from him I knew they could be serious, but I didn't want to go to the police about it. It was a question of wait-and-see, and hoping things might die down.

In the end they did. When he was out, I ran into him at a bar and there were no problems at all. He seemed to get that it was best to let it go and move quietly on.

Summer arrived and training went up a level, as we had started to prep for the next meeting. Andreas had organised sparring partners suited to the coming fight. Stockholm Shoot was crawling with Matyushenko clones for those few weeks, all of them trying to beat the shit out of me.

Things were working well in Stockholm, but I still felt I had to get back to San Diego. It wasn't only that the coaching and opposition were good there, I needed to get away from my everyday life. If you are warming up for a big fight you have to step outside your comfort zone. Anything that lets you relax or feel good is potentially fatal. Another advantage to finishing our prep in California was that we wouldn't have to deal with the time difference for the fight itself.

Before I left, I had to go and visit Wiggo in Köping. When I arrived you could see how ill he really was. Despite his condition he still talked to me in the same way, and he held his usual prayer session. It was important to me.

A few days later I flew to San Diego by myself. Andreas was going to come a bit later and coach me at Alliance for the final week. By this time I knew everyone there fairly well, and Eric Del Fierro was someone I could rely on one hundred per cent. He had already pushed my wrestling a long way and he could see my strengths and weaknesses in a way few other people did.

I had been at Alliance less than a week when he came up to me with a furrowed brow. I asked what was up and he told me he had just heard that Matyushenko had picked up an injury in training.

He'd had to cancel our fight. This is something we all have to contend with; it can happen to you or your opponent at any time. In the training camps we do to prep for fights you have to go all in and you always risk injury. There is no other way to do it, but obviously it is still frustrating when it happens.

I stared at Eric and felt the energy drain from my body. It was up to UFC to try and find a well-ranked replacement for Matyushenko. It had to be someone prepared to fight at short notice, and that isn't usually a problem, as most fighters are keen not to lose their contracts. At this level it is often so long between fights that you take the chances you're given, even if you are not entirely ready. Sometimes fighters will jump in to replace an injured UFC guy with as little as two or three days' notice.

Soon we got news that they had found a replacement, the American Matt 'The Hammer' Hamill, who debuted in UFC in 2006 and had a number of victories under his belt. Hamill was at least as good an opponent and, like the Belarussian he replaced, a good wrestler. Even so, everyone is different and has a different style or specialism, so I basically had to start from scratch, not least mentally. Things felt kind of tough right then. The only consolation was that me and Hamill both had the same short timespan to gear up against fighters that could imitate us. One of the things that marked Hamill out was that he had been deaf since birth. I tried to imagine what it was like not to hear the crowd or the coaches shouting. Would it calm him down? Would he be more focused? Or was it a real disadvantage?

Eric, Phil Davis, Dominick Cruz, Jared Platt, Brandon Vera and the others at the gym helped me realign my training. We watched videos of Hamill and drew up strategies and a game plan as we trained. Brandon said he felt sorry for Hamill and looked forward to the look on the guy's face as I landed my first punch. According to Brandon, even a jab from me was explosive.

The training camp was over and when me, Eric and Phil left

Alliance I was in the right frame of mind. I was wired for the fight, and when you have come through all the prep, then all you want is to get it chalked off. All your focus is on one thing, but annoyingly you have to think about loads of other stuff before the fight itself. In Philly there were press conferences, interviews and a load of other media stuff. I also needed to shed a few kilos to get under the weight limit and I had to run and run on the treadmill in a sweat suit.

Mum and my sister came over for the fight, and it was good to see them there. After the weigh-in we all went to a restaurant with my Swedish MMA friend, Akira Corassani. I ate myself back to life with a desperation that made Elina chuckle. She knows me so well that she could see how much I had suffered losing the weight that past week, because she knows I love eating, preferably as unhealthily as possible.

The night after, it was time for the fight, but as I walked into the arena I didn't give the change in opponent a second thought. As soon as the fight started I carried out my revised game plan and made sure Matt didn't have a chance to take a bite out of me. I moved and moved, smacking him whenever I saw an opening. Towards the end of the first round he managed to catch me on my right eyebrow, but I hardly felt it. It was only the sensation of blood on my cheek that told me he had made contact.

In the second round he tried and failed to take me down.

I got a few kicks away, following them up with a jab and two uppercuts to put him on the floor. The blood from my eyebrow ran into my mouth and tasted of metal. I pummelled him and went at him with my elbow as I got on top, and with a minute left the ref stopped the fight.

I looked at Andreas and Eric in my corner of the ring. They had their arms in the air. I could hardly believe it was happening; I had beaten one of the top fighters in my class, and I had done it so convincingly that it sent out a message to all the guys ranked higher than me.

The blond Swede was coming.

Chapter 12
New Year Fireworks in Vegas

I went on a diet. No drink, no tobacco, no sex, and hardly any going out. It was like being a monk in the worst place in the world to be one.

Wins always make you feel good, but some of them make you feel like magic. The victory against Matt Hamill was one of the latter. When I got back to Stockholm I found out that I had moved up a few rungs on the ladder and was now the highest-ranked Swede. I also found out that the defeat had been such a blow to The Hammer he was going to hang up his gloves.

As usual I was feeling sore, but not injured really. The truth is you pick up more injuries from training than from the fights, which comes as a surprise to a lot of people. A lot of those who criticise the sport don't get that you train yourself to defend as much as you do to attack. When you take a punch that puts you on the floor, the ref is over so quick that there's rarely a chance to sustain any real injuries. There's a bit of blood, of course, and the bruises and swelling you pick up on your face would worry any mother (my mum sits with her hands over her eyes for most of my fights); but it always looks much worse than it actually is, and you can usually pick yourself up, no problem.

You might be tired, but you have to get back to training sharpish, in part because your physical condition can worsen quickly and you never know when UFC will ring with another fight for you. Sometimes you only have to wait a few weeks before people start talking about who your next opponent will be. There is a whole lot of tactical thinking, negotiation and game-playing behind all of that. I'm grateful I don't have to do it myself and that I have managers who can sort it out for me.

All I could do now was keep training at Stockholm Shoot and hope for an even higher-ranked fighter to face off against. I had a 12–1 win ratio and anyone could see it was well-earned.

Things were going well between me and Anna. Being with a fighter is a unique experience. You need strong nerves and you can't worry about things you have no control over. You have to try and be that way, at least, otherwise you're done for. Anna was hardy and could take it – I saw that straight away – and we had started to discuss getting a proper apartment together. The Rågsved flat was Jimmy's, and even if he seemed very attached to Singapore, it felt like time to move on. I looked around and through some contacts I got hold of a little two-room place in Västertorp, a touch nearer the city. Soon we were in a van driving through Stockholm's south-side. The area was quiet, which suited me. I'm a country boy at heart and I like a bit of nature around me.

We got set up quickly, and it turned out to be a good autumn for the most part. Training went well and I didn't pick up any injuries, and then Manos popped up one day with some good news.

As usual there had been a lot of chat about who I would face, but eventually we settled back on Vladimir Matyushenko, the same guy I was going to fight back in the summer before he got injured. It felt like a good match-up, given I had spent all those months sparring with guys who had the same fighting style. He was already in my sights, you could say.

The fight was part of a UFC event on 30 December in Las Vegas. I had dreamed of fighting there because Vegas is such a classic venue for boxing and MMA.

'But wait,' I said to Manos. 'Isn't that the day before New Year?'

'Yep,' he replied. 'We'll be seeing in the new year in Vegas! Maybe Christmas, too.'

That thought didn't seem quite as appealing as the town and the fight did. I usually spent Christmas at home with Mum, and I knew it would feel weird to miss out and not go home that year.

Anna wasn't too happy, either, when I told her I'd be missing Christmas.

Like we always did, I began my prep at Stockholm Shoot and made sure Wiggo had time to bless me before me and Andreas jetted over to Alliance in San Diego. Eric, Phil and the rest of the team there were going to give me another masterclass in grappling and wrestling. In return they got treated to top-class coaching from

Andreas, who by now had established himself as one of the top boxing guys in the world.

Alliance began to feel like a second home. I liked the city as well. It was an easy life, and this time me and Andreas were put up in a boat that belonged to my sponsors Bad Boy, moored in a harbour on the Coronado peninsula.

It was amazing watching the sun go up and down over the horizon, and waking up to the sound of seagulls each morning. In the evenings, when I had been going hard at the gym for six or seven hours, it was nice to simply kick back in the cabin in front of a film. One night we watched a horror film and it reminded me of when I was six or seven and slept over at a friend's for the first time. His name was also Andreas, and he was two years older.

We met because his dad Benny used to come to the farm in Boda. We had sixty cows then and Benny was a casual worker like Mum, who would come and milk them. Andreas and me screamed off into the woods or around the farmyard as soon as we had the chance, and sometimes we would have sleepovers afterwards. It worked fine when Andreas came to our place, but if I went to his there were always problems, because I was so afraid of the dark. It didn't help that we stayed up late watching horror flicks. I've always liked stuff that gives me a fright, but when it was time to turn out the lights, I couldn't sleep.

Old houses like the one at their farm creak and squeak at night, so Andreas's parents would often find themselves ringing Mum in the middle of the night so she could come and get me. There was one time she didn't, when it was quite late. Everyone except me was sleeping, and because I had already been asleep for what felt like ages I suddenly needed to go to the toilet. The problem was that the toilet was in their cellar, and going downstairs in the dark wasn't an option. Waking up Andreas or his parents to come with me wasn't a viable alternative, so I had no choice but to wet myself.

'Why is the bed wet?' he sniggered.

I desperately tried to think of an answer. The best I could do was, 'It must have been the cat!'

In San Diego sleeping was no problem. When you've trained hard all day, you fall asleep like a man knocked unconscious. You also know you have to be up early to go through it all again the following day. It was hard going, but the camp went surprisingly well. I picked up no injuries and Matyushenko managed not to get any either. After celebrating a low-key and diet-friendly Swedish Christmas on the boat with Anna and Andreas, we got in the hire car and drove up to Las Vegas. Eric, Phil and the English fighter Ross Pearson, who had trained with us at Alliance and also had a fight on the bill, followed in another car. Ross was a featherweight and was going to be on the undercard.

For the first time my fight was part of the main bill. It felt big. To go to Vegas was just as seminal, or more simply it was insane, because the whole town is insane. That's especially the case when you're not there to do what it does best – gamble and party till you drop. I went on a diet. No drink, no tobacco, no sex, and hardly any going out. It was like being a monk in the worst place in the world to be one. I did my media stuff for UFC, and spent the rest of the time in the hotel room I shared with Andreas and Manos.

The night before I fight I usually eat dinner with Mum and Elina, but annoyingly I had mixed up my dates when I booked the plane tickets for them and they had ended up stuck at Arlanda airport in Stockholm. Instead I ended up shovelling down food alongside Andreas and Manos.

Breakfast and lunch the following morning were also utter carnage. That is how Vegas works. You can't take the hotel buffets lightly, and after the obligatory crash diet before the weigh-in my body was screaming for carbs.

The MGM Grand Arena is hallowed ground. Tyson and Mayweather have fought there, and now it was my turn. Put bluntly, it was unreal.

I warmed up in the changing rooms in good time. I went through the game plan one last time with Andreas and Eric. Then it was suddenly time to step out. The arena was bigger than I'd expected, and the size of the crowd was unbelievable. Luckily I could ignore most of it – if you can't shut out the noise, then it is easy to lose your sharpness. You can't be overexcited or emotional either when you walk in. Being angry is a no-no, because it'll undermine you as soon as the fight starts. Being able to go in as cold as ice is one of my greatest strengths as a fighter. That night as I climbed into the Octagon and heard the ref shout 'Fight!' everything felt right.

I put myself in the middle of the cage and tried to get a feel for him. Matyushenko got a right-hander ready and came towards me. Instinctively I gave him a left-hand jab and got him right on the chin. Matyushenko fell as if I had smacked him with an axe, and all that was left for me to do was finish him with a few blows on the floor.

When I climbed out, the Octagon people seemed to love what I had done. Someone who was obviously impressed was Dana White, president of UFC. Straight after the event he said publicly that I was a fighter to reckon with and told the press I deserved higher-ranked opposition next time around. I wanted nothing else.

Back in Stockholm the victory also created a bit of a buzz, not least in the press. MMA was still a long way from being socially acceptable in Sweden, and a lot of people seemed to think that what me and my colleagues did was ugly, repulsive violence. No top magazines wanted to interview me and there was no space for me on the family-friendly TV shows. Even the sports news didn't feature me, but I got a mention in some of the smaller newspapers in a small breakthrough for my profile. To be honest, press coverage wasn't a big thing for me; all I wanted to do was get a new fight organised, ideally before the summer.

Soon after I got back to training at Stockholm Shoot, which was now called Nexus, I got a piece of news that hit me like a bomb:

UFC had decided to match me up with Little Nog – Antonio Rogério Nogueira. He was a Brazilian, younger brother of the much bigger Minotauro. Unlike his brother, Little Nog hadn't won a title in both Pride and UFC, but he was a fierce fighter and had claimed some big scalps, including Alistair Overeem and Dan Henderson. Before my last fight in Vegas, he had taken down the legendary Tito Ortiz in the first round. In some ways he was as impressive an opponent for me as his big brother.

The fight was going to be top of the card at the first event UFC had ever held in Sweden. What's more, it was going to be at the massive Stockholm Globe Arena. It felt unreal when Manos told me. My head couldn't quite take it all in. The event was called UFC Sweden and was happening on 14 April, which meant I had to get started straight away. Usually Andreas would divide my prep into three stages: first was strength building, then endurance, and finally agility. Right then we didn't have time for all three, so we skipped stage one and went straight to the endurance stuff.

As usual we were due to do four weeks in Stockholm and another four with the Alliance boys in San Diego. I was to finish up with a few weeks at home with Mum. She and Kalle had split up, and she had got herself an old country house called Sörby, where she ran a bed-and-breakfast together with her new partner, Jarmo.

Jarmo had got some friends in and built a gym for me in one of their outbuildings. The ring and all the gear I had got from a company called Nordic Fighter in Örebro as sponsorship. It was the perfect place to train with Andreas and my sparring partners in peace and quiet, letting my body adjust to Swedish time.

Before we could do anything, there was hard work to be done at Nexus. Andreas and Manos ensured a steady stream of southpaw, or left-handed, boxers to face me. We needed them because Little Nog was left-handed. They also got one of the world's best Thai boxers over to get me ready for my opponent's unorthodox style, a technically skilled fighter and dangerous because he was so hard to predict. I had the best training competition and coaches who knew what they were doing. Alongside Andreas, I had the Swedes Max Philipsson and Jesper Hallberg, and in the US I could look forward to the guiding hand of Eric Del Fierro to test my wrestling skills once again.

Anna had hoped she might have me to herself for a while when I got back from Vegas. That wasn't how it turned out, however, because the fights were so close together I had almost no downtime at all. If she was upset about how things were, she hid it well, and instead she did what she could to make things easier for me, something I really appreciated. Prepping for a fight can be so intense that you need the everyday stuff to go like clockwork. You can't start doing the cleaning when you get home from the gym of an evening. I'm usually so exhausted I just fall onto the sofa in a heap.

Chapter 13

UFC Sweden

I felt grateful as I sat there and looked at him. There lay the man who had guided me and so many others through the darkest of moments, a beacon of light as I fell into the shadows. Without him there would be an indescribable emptiness in my life.

The plan had been for me and Andreas to carry on our prep at Alliance in San Diego. Instead we were headed back to Las Vegas, all because of UFC's reality show *The Ultimate Fighter*. The new series was being filmed in Vegas and as usual there were going to be two teams of relative unknowns yet to make their breakthrough. This time they had a group of lightweights, who would go up against each other in a knockout tournament. After weeks of fighting the winner ended up with a fat cheque and a UFC contract.

It was a good show I liked to watch myself, but one of the teams was being coached by my Alliance buddy Dominick Cruz. He was being assisted by Phil Davis and Eric Del Fierro. Eric in particular had grown in importance for me during my training, and he said he would always help me if ever I pitched up at his door. They had already started the recording and were consumed by it. They were going to be TV stars, and that would make anyone run away with themselves. I was mostly jet-lagged and could hardly hear what Manos was saying when he rang me. I asked him to repeat what he had said.

'I've some good news and some bad news,' he said.

My stomach tightened. I hate uncertainty.

'Come on, tell me,' I said.

'You sold out the whole Globe Arena in three hours. Never before in the history of UFC has an event sold that quick.'

'Fuck,' I said. 'And the bad news?'

'Little Nog is injured. He's out.'

I took a deep breath, but before I had time to say anything else Manos told me what I wanted to know:

'You're going to fight Thiago Silva instead.'

'Thiago Silva!' I shouted, as happy as I had been disappointed only seconds before. It is a rollercoaster to lose an opponent one minute and get a new one the next. Silva was also Brazilian, and he was well-established with a win record of 14–2. He was a more orthodox fighter than Little Nog and strong on the ground. I needed to focus on my agility to keep him at a distance. On the upside he was less technically accomplished than Little Nog, but as always at that level it wasn't something you dwelt on. In MMA absolutely anything can happen, and when it does it can all be over very quickly. You end up on the mat not knowing what the hell went wrong.

The only guys who had managed to stop Silva before were Lyoto Machida and Rashad Evans. That said a lot. This guy was deadly, and even though I was fighting on home turf, I knew it would be tough.

It was just as tough being back in limbo again. You work hard and prepare yourself to meet one guy with very particular moves, devoting hours and hours to it and sparring with similar opponents as much as you possibly can. It costs blood, sweat, money, and sometimes even tears of doubt, and then someone comes and tells you it's all off.

That's when it helps to have a coach who can calm you down and motivate you to come back for another bite. Andreas told me the obvious: we had to come up with a new game plan based on Thiago's strengths and weaknesses, prepping as meticulously and with the same focus as before.

It was easier said than done in that crazy city. Vegas is fun to be in for a few days, but after a while it is too much. There's nothing natural or real there at all. In the long term it is a frustrating experience, especially for someone like me.

After three weeks in Vegas I was going mad. I also seemed to have sand in my mouth the whole time, I mean there was sand everywhere. In my hair, in my clothes, in the bed, in the shower and in the food. I literally have no idea how people can live there full time.

Travelling from Vegas to Sweden is a long trip, but it wasn't the marathon flight that made me break down when me and Andreas got to Mum's in Sörby. It was a total contrast with the gambling metropolis, you can't imagine two more different places. The calm and the silence knocked me out completely and I slept twelve hours straight. I felt a lot better after that, especially with some of Mum's cooking inside me.

Some people probably think I'm an emotionally strong person, but they should meet my mum and grandma. Those two women are like rocks.

There were two weeks to go until the fight and I felt calmer than ever before. Maybe it was because I was at home amongst people I loved, maybe it was because I had done all I could. There's nothing worse than climbing into that cage and worrying about something; whether or not you are in top form or if the training was as good as it could have been. Everything has to feel right, then you can focus solely on the fight itself.

It was great to be able to train at home like we did. In the outbuilding at Mum's there was everything me and Andreas needed. The ring was as big as the one in which I would compete in Stockholm, and the place was fully equipped. I could also bring in as many guys as I wanted to train against, because there was endless space in the house. Mum had bought it after harbouring a dream for many years to run a guest house. The place had been really run down when she took it over, but Perra had helped her do it up. He had also helped build the training gym I was using.

Even at that late point in the training plan you can't hold back to try and avoid injuries. I went all in as I warmed up against a string of fighters that included MMA veteran Tor Troéng and Papy Abedi, who had a fight tabled at the Globe himself.

We had a good time in Sörby and the sessions were fun. Those final few days are more important than you might think, because that's what you take with you into the fight itself. It might sound obvious, but before big fights in particular, the pressure can easily show in the form of irritableness and bad moods.

After one of our Sörby training sessions I got in the car and drove to Köping to see Wiggo. It was even clearer to me how ill he was, because it had been a while since we last met. I grasped that he didn't have much time left, and that really hit me. How was I supposed to get by when he was gone? Wiggo had supported me and believed in me when I was at my lowest ebb. Ever since we first met he had been there when I needed him. When I was younger me and a lot of other guys from gangs could pitch up at his place and just sit there drinking coffee in the lounge. He got what we were about and I felt grateful as I sat there and looked at him. There lay the man who had guided me and so many others through the darkest of moments, a beacon of light as I fell into the shadows. Without him there would be an indescribable emptiness in my life.

It was quiet but the days raced by in Sörby, and soon it was time to leave for Stockholm and the obligatory PR stuff we had to do before the event. There were more interviews than usual, and more fan meet-ups, including an open training session at a gym in the city. Me and Andreas did a bit of light boxing, and a few of the other fighters on the event's main card showed off their skills. Those sessions have zero value in terms of training but are important marketing tactics and that is part of the whole game. All you have to do is smile and do what you are supposed to, exactly as it is written down in the contract. The thing is, trying to look happy and outgoing in those kinds of situations is not always easy – you've already trained to death and you are mostly frustrated, on a diet, and nervous about a fight that could make or break your career.

Eventually Saturday came. The Globe was packed. I couldn't even get tickets for my own family, it was insane. It was like MMA had suddenly gone mainstream in Sweden there and then, and I rode into that arena on a wave. The cheers of the crowd were deafening. I had more reason than usual not to lose.

Earlier in the evening my mate Reza 'Mad Dog' Madadi had driven the crowd wild when he guillotined his opponent in the second round. I loved that man to bits and I sure didn't want to do worse when I climbed into the Octagon with the same tunnel vision as always.

In my career I have only ever felt impressed or starstruck by two opponents. Thiago Silva was not one of them, and after we had got a feel for one another my nervousness vanished. It was time to get to work.

I landed a few explosive blows and was close to finishing him in the first round. For a split second I thought the Globe was about to take off, the crowd were cheering so loud. Silva can take it, though, and he managed to get up again. Halfway through the second round he hit me with his right and left me wobbling.

At times like that you have to stay calm until your brain kicks back in. That was when the huge crowd came in handy. For the first time ever I was out of reach of my coach, who was drowned out. The only sound in my ears was 12,000 people screaming, 'Hit him, hit him!'

I took control again with jabs, uppercuts and a few blows with the knee. It was as if Silva didn't know how to deal with me or how he should respond. In the break between rounds two and three I knew I had won the first two. I also knew Silva would be getting desperate and would try and take risks. His only chance of winning was to finish me completely. My footwork was good and I managed to stay out of his way every time he took a swing at me. I could have gone at him a little harder, but when you know you are in front it is easier to play it carefully. As it turned out I won the third round, too, as all three judges decided I had bested him. I don't need to explain how great it felt to stand there in a packed Globe and put my arms in the air. I was just one big smile, and afterwards I even enjoyed the press conference we gave. I felt deep relief at living up to people's expectations as well. Sometimes the pressure can be as tough as the fight.

For twelve days after, we had no training. The body needs time to recover. If you're unlucky and get injured then it needs even longer for rehabilitation, but I felt pretty good. I revelled in my victory and the fact that afterwards Dana White said I was deserving of a match-up with a top-five fighter.

There was also my bank account. When I checked my balance a few days later I could hardly believe my eyes. Last time I'd checked I had 700 kronor in it, now I had half a million. Manos had said I would get a UFC bonus because I had won a big event, but this was insane. Half a million! I had to call Manos to check it was true. He laughed and told me that if I thought money was a burden I should give it all to someone else.

People who have always had money can't really understand what it feels like to suddenly be rich. I decided to put some of the prize money towards two pedigree dogs, but when I told Perra my plans he said it sounded like a bad idea. He gave me the laboured look I know so well and said, 'Jesus, man, do you know what you're getting into there? Those dogs will take up all your time and you'll be away travelling. Think about it.'

I shrugged. 'You're exaggerating. When I'm away Anna can look after them. It'll work out,' I told him.

Anna was actually quite keen, so I used my time off from training to drive down to Amsterdam (seventeen hours each way) to get two American Bully dogs I had chosen. These aren't lapdogs we're talking about, but little bags of muscle. Even though they look terrifying to some people, they are actually great family pets.

They were beautiful when I first saw them. Both had great breeding histories and were champions through and through. That meant I would make my money back once I had produced a litter or two of puppies. The bitch, called Sativa, cost 35,000 and the male was called Ghost. He cost me double, but I didn't hesitate a second. An American Bully is the best possible companion for someone like me, and I was overjoyed when I got back to Västertorp with them. It was also nice to see how quickly Perra was won over when he set eyes on them. All talk of not having the time quickly disappeared.

Everything was going well. I was enjoying life with Anna and we had two sweet little monsters of dogs to raise and look after. They ate like there was no tomorrow, and needed to be taken out constantly. A lot of the time we ended up driving out to Mum's with them, where they had the space to run around.

Soon I was back in training at Nexus and doing my daily sessions with Andreas, Jesper, Max and the other coaches. It also felt fantastic to be financially carefree for the first time ever. With the sponsors I had done deals with, I didn't have to worry any more.

It was already autumn when we got news of a new fight. As per usual it was Manos who was the messenger, and as usual he dragged it out to see my reaction.

'C'mon!' I said. 'Tell me!'

'Shogun.'

'You're fucking joking.'

Manos shook his head and smiled.

This was it. I was going to fight the Brazilian Maurício 'Shogun' Rua, who me and Carlos used to watch on YouTube back when I lived at the Family. He was a living legend and had been light-heavyweight UFC champion before he lost the title to Jon Jones. That summer he had destroyed my training buddy Brandon Vera at a UFC event in LA. I had to ring Carlos, who was as ecstatic about the news as I was. I was on the threshold of what we had talked about six years before, something I had dismissed as impossible at the time.

Me and Andreas started planning our prep straight away. The fight was in Seattle on 8 December, so we decided to finish up the training camp with some time at Alliance. I started to prepare mentally and was in a better frame of mind than ever before when I got a call from Perra. It was the morning of 24 September. In as much as I could hear his voice, I understood what it was about. Wiggo was gone.

In his customary way Wiggo had opened his home to others and invited an addict to sleep on his sofa. Before they had gone to bed for the night Wiggo had knelt to pray, but only had time to say a few words before he collapsed. Through my shock I thought what a fitting death it was for him. He lived the Christian message of love and compassion, and he had died with that same message on his lips.

Even though I knew it was coming, I was still totally unprepared for it. I also felt lost. Who would help me in my moments of doubt? Who would be my spiritual guide? Who would bless me before my fight against Shogun?

Even though I knew Wiggo would have wanted me to go on as usual, it was a few days before I made it back into the gym.

At the funeral on 19 October in Saint Mary's church in Köping there were hundreds of us gathered, including a group of Methodist pastors like Wiggo from all over Scandinavia. Me and Perra carried the coffin together with Wiggo's relatives. They knew me and Perra had been close to him, and Perra had almost been like a son to him, caring for him as his illness worsened. Both of them were orphans in their own ways, as Wiggo had also grown up in a home and Perra had been shipped from family to family like a box of junk.

Me and Perra were there for each other right then, and he promised me that he would fill Wiggo's shoes and pray for me before each meeting. During the moment of remembrance at the church in Tunadal, after the burial, people said many kind things about Wiggo – all of them true.

Chapter 14
Shogun

s I sat in the changing room and had my hands bandaged that nervousness crept up on me again, even though I had learned to keep my emotions in check by then. When I was younger it had been different, but I dealt with it better than some other guys, who would get so scared they would vomit.

At the start of November, a few weeks after we had buried Wiggo, me and Andreas flew back to San Diego. Though I had been a bit nervous about my opponent, it vanished as soon as we got down to training at the gym in Chula Vista. I was in safe hands, and those boys made me laugh. Phil Davis, in particular, can really lift the mood in a room. When we wrestled each other, we were like two brothers having a play-fight. We had a great time together, and I remember thinking how weird it would be if Dana White suddenly decided we would fight each other again for real. How on earth can you fight a friend like that?

Apart from two training sessions each day and five rounds of sparring, pre-fight interviews had become part of the prep routine. I also had to turn up at certain events for my sponsors, though that could be fun. A few months before, I'd taken part in a multisport challenge organised by Unibet. I had competed at tug-of-war and wrestling with the football legends Glenn Hysén and Tomas Brolin, as well as the pro hockey player Victor Hedman. Me and Glenn had even got in the ring together for a bit of boxing.

It was less fun being pushed to the point of vomiting on the treadmill as Andreas stood next to me with a stopwatch shouting, 'Run like a feather!' Before I fell asleep at night the fight would suddenly be on my mind. It was unavoidable; I was about to meet one of my idols. He was also a real predator or, as Andreas put it, 'a better version of Thiago Silva'. It was an accurate description, and he had an insane knockout punch and a fighting heart. This was going to be a baptism of fire.

The day of the UFC event got nearer, and me and the team flew up to Seattle to do some photoshoots and press conferences with Dana White. I sat up straight in my seat when Dana answered one question by saying the winner of my fight would be given the chance to take the title off Jon Jones. At the open training afterwards, the prospect refused to vanish from my thoughts.

Usually UFC events take place in the evening and the main fight is late on. But this time I did my walkout at six p.m. The whole thing was arranged so the broadcasters could maximise their advertising revenue, but it felt strange setting off for the Key Arena straight after lunch to get ready for the fight.

As I sat in the changing room and had my hands bandaged, that nervousness crept up on me again, although I had learned to keep my emotions in check by then. When I was younger it had been different, but I dealt with it better than some other guys, who would get so scared they would vomit. There are a fair few fighters who have had to throw in the towel because their nerves go. Just because you're a useful fighter in the gym or on the street, it doesn't mean you can take the pressure of a UFC event in front of a crowd of thousands of screaming fans.

It was time for the fight. In my whole career, there have been only two opponents I've had much respect for, and this guy was without doubt one of them. Even so, the fight had hardly got going before I had Shogun on the ground and started pounding him. He responded by getting my legs in a lock, but I wriggled out without much trouble. Then I got him down again and found myself on the floor as well. I forced myself up, jabbed him with my knee and then suddenly the first round was over. In the second round Shogun went in hard with his right and started taking crazy swings at me. But in the middle of the round I took him down again, and even managed to knee him in the face a few times. My jabs were also working, and by the end of the round he looked almost broken.

In the third I carried on much as before. I put him on the floor twice and got him in a guard. Shogun had nothing more to come at me with. I dominated the fight and towards the end of the third round I put a kick straight onto his chin that sent him tumbling again. When the fight was over, I had twice as many punches on him as he had on me.

When all the journalists asked me how it felt afterwards, I didn't know how to respond. It is easy to speak in clichés, to say words that don't really do justice to how you feel inside. But I had just beaten one of my idols and climbed into the world top five in my weight class. That kind of tells you all you need to know.

Andreas had started to tire of doing other people's bidding for low wages and was frustrated at not being able to follow his own path. It led him and Manos to open a gym with a few other guys called Allstars Training Centre on Hagagatan in central Stockholm. In no time at all they had all the top Swedish fighters signed up.

Just like at Alliance, I could get all the inspiration and opposition I needed there. The coaches were great, too. There was Andreas, but I also had access to the kickboxer Jocke Karlsson, a guy called Alan 'Finfou' Nascimento, who taught me grappling and Brazilian jiu-jitsu, and the wrestler Jesper Hallberg. It couldn't get any better, or so I thought. Soon UFC were in touch again and wanted me to fight Gegard Mousasi at a new event at the Globe Arena. Mousasi had been successful in a rival competition called Strikeforce and won the light-heavyweight title. UFC had bought up and then closed down Strikeforce, so Mousasi and a string of other fighters had suddenly ended up in the UFC instead. Dana White had more or less promised me a title fight, but Jon Jones already had a fixture arranged against Chael Sonnen. To keep myself going, I decided together with Andreas and Manos to take the fight. I also felt exhilarated at the prospect of fighting in front of a hometown crowd again.

The positive atmosphere at Allstars pumped me up and we decided to run our entire pre-fight camp there. To begin with training was fun, but the nearer we got to the fight day, the harder I was pushed. By the end it was pure pain. Even when it is impossible and you want to drop everything, go home and eat chocolate on the sofa, you know you'll get the payoff if you can hold out a little bit longer. That was why it was such a catastrophe when it happened: a week before the fight I got a cut to my face in sparring and began to bleed heavily.

When you get an injury that close to a fight, you have to tell the Swedish MMA association straight away. Andreas rang them and soon a doctor came down who told me the fight was not going to happen.

All the air went out of me. These things happen, but I felt it was my fault. I thought I had to take the blame for all the people who would feel disappointed now. The most disappointed person of all, of course, was me.

My friend and training partner Ilir Latifi jumped in to replace me. It was his UFC debut and Ilir put on a good show that night, earning a fair bit of respect for his performance, but ended up losing on points.

After the cancelled fight I fell into a bit of a hole. Manos also seemed very down. He had worked incredibly hard in the run-up to the event and hardly slept. Manos had become friendly with a guy called Tomas Ghassemi, who worked with PR and marketing in Dubai and the States. Tomas had seen how hard Manos was pushing himself and still not getting everything done, so he'd offered his services. Soon afterwards, they had started to work together on a trial basis.

However hard I tried, I could not motivate myself to get back into training again. It felt like the cancelled fight had been a defeat. Then suddenly something entirely unexpected happened – the reigning champion, Jon Jones, started to talk shit about me on Twitter. He probably saw me as easy pickings and wanted to get me riled up before a potential fight, so fairly soon the banter was flowing. Around then I also got a request to go to Moscow and fight at an event organised by some super-rich oligarch. Manos did not have time to come along, so I was going with Majdi from Allstars instead. The night before we left, I happened to look at the fight card. I rang Manos immediately.

'Know who else is going to be in Moscow?'

'Nope.'

'Jones.'

'Great. Challenge him.'

I did as Manos told me. In front of a load of Russian VIPs and other fighters, me and Jones engaged in a staredown. I said he looked afraid. Next day on Twitter I said he would remain unbeaten as long as he kept fighting short guys, but that things would be different if he and I got in the ring. It was cheeky, but it was true.

Unfortunately Jones injured his foot in the fight against Chael Sonnen, and people were saying it could take six months before he was ready to go again. It meant we still had no idea if I would ever get to fight him. I'm not exaggerating when I say I waited on tenterhooks every single day for news from UFC. When it finally came the week before midsummer it was one of the happiest moments of my life.

Suddenly training seemed easier, and when I took a break to celebrate midsummer out in the country with Mum and my family, I took the opportunity to do something I had wanted to do for a long time: I got baptised. I thought it would be a good thing for me, but also a fine way to pay my respects to Wiggo. It was good timing as well; I was about to take on my biggest ever challenge and I needed all the strength I could muster.

I had already been baptised as a kid, but when you do it as an adult it is more of a commitment. Me, Anna and Perra went out to a nice spot on Lake Mälaren, where we met up with Mum, Grandma and the rest of the family. Then I waded into the still-cold water and the pastor put my head under. When you baptise an adult you immerse the whole body, washing away all your old sins. Anna did it, too, and it felt right. We could share the experience and share our faith.

All title fights are five rounds of five minutes each, and even though UFC claim they want it to be decisive for the sake of the crowd, the title bouts often end up running out of time. A champion simply doesn't want to risk losing his belt, so you end up thinking tactically.

In my training camps we would normally go five rounds in sparring, so this time we did seven. My fighting style, footwork and emphasis on boxing means I have to be in peak condition the whole time. To make sure that was the case, Andreas forced me to run up the hill in Hammarby until I fell on the ground and vomited. At Allstars the physical training was the hardest I had ever done. Like everyone I don't like discomfort, but I had a goal to reach and was ready to do anything that would get me there. It was pure hell, but I could see that title belt in front of me the whole time and that pushed me on.

When it was time to move training to San Diego, I did my usual thing and drove out to Mum and Grandma in Sörby to say goodbye before I left. All three of us sat in Grandma's kitchen and I stroked her ginger-striped cat, who had been given the name Wiggo after my mentor. I really missed him, and wished he could have blessed me like he used to before my fights. I knew Grandma, Perra and the others back home would still be saying prayers for me, and as I stood in the doorway before leaving, Grandma looked me straight in the eyes and said, 'God bless your opponent, Alex, but you have to beat him!'

I promised her I would.

Chapter 15
Jon 'Bones' Jones

ones played his mind games the whole time. One day we were best buddies and he asked me how I was doing, the next he made out-of-order jokes and threw me long looks.

When I get to the end of a training camp before a fight I am always emotional. If I've had a bad day in training I can lose it with Andreas or cry in frustration. I am an extremely bad loser, even in training, and I have to avenge even the smallest defeat as soon as possible.

Manos, Tomas, Andreas, Jimmy and all the others close to me know how I work. They also know how to deal with me, even if they do like to mess me about for a laugh sometimes.

When we checked into the Toronto Hilton on 18 September 2013 everyone was behaving themselves. There was this air of seriousness compared to how it usually was before my fights.

Like we always did, me and Manos shared a room, and from what I remember we both went out like a light that evening.

The morning after, it was time for all the press stuff. As we were close to weigh-in I had stopped eating or drinking, and I went straight from the room to reception. Manos meanwhile had a leisurely hotel breakfast by himself.

While I was waiting I was swamped with people looking for photos and autographs. All that stuff was still quite new to me. I had got attention when I beat Thiago Silva in Stockholm, and people came up and asked me for autographs in Sweden now and then, but this was different.

Eventually Manos appeared and we went to the entrance, where we were met by a girl from UFC. She told us to jump in a white van that would take us to the Shangri La hotel where all the events were taking place. First in the diary was a press conference featuring me and Jones.

To create interest in the fight UFC had sent us on a world press tour to a load of different countries. Jones played his mind games the whole time. One day we were best buddies and he asked me how I was doing, the next he made out-of-order jokes and threw me long looks. This was our final press conference and he picked up his phone and started filming me when we were doing our staredown. Everything was designed to psyche me out. I can tell you he didn't succeed, he just seemed kind of ridiculous. I had respect for him as a fighter, though, and for the second time in my life ever, I actually felt a bit starstruck. I mean, this guy was pound-for-pound the best fighter in the world, demolishing guys left, right, and centre. There was also a lot of hype about him. He was not a normal guy; he didn't bleed, he was deadly, and more. I heard it all, and it affected me.

When the press conference was over and all the media stuff was done with it was already late afternoon. However, I couldn't rest because I had to get rid of the last ounces of fluid from my body for the weigh-in. You can usually get rid of two kilos if you do it right. So me and Andreas went down to the hotel gym to do 10K on the treadmill in a sweat suit. People who don't know how this industry works think the fight is the hard bit, but nothing could be further from the truth. The fight is the reward for all the pain you go through beforehand.

Because it was September and still fairly warm in Toronto they held the weigh-in outdoors in Maple Leaf Square. Me and Andreas went down on the UFC bus shortly after five. There were loads of people in the square, and next to the stage a marquee had been set up where we were to wait until we were called up.

Jones was already there, jumping up and down in time to the music on his headphones. 'Oh baby, Oh baby,' he was singing.

Me and Andreas just looked at each other and went over to the side to wait until we were needed. There is a whole lot of waiting before each fight and it can be unbearable. At long last I was called up to the stage, together with Andreas.

Even if you know you are the right weight for the fight there is always a bit of tension before the weigh-in. But the weight-loss trick had worked as it was supposed to, so all that was left was one final staredown.

One of the ways Jones tries to unsettle his opponents is not to look them in the eyes when it comes to the staredown. If you can look into someone's eyes you know their deal, but if your opponent stares at the ceiling they could be anything from hard as nails to scared for their life. By this point I was past caring. All I wanted to do was get him in the cage and finish the job.

When I got on the bus back to the hotel I was given food replacement intravenously so I could recover from the intensive weight loss. Then I was allowed to get stuck into the huge hamburger Andreas had got for me. It is hard to describe how good it tasted. I think maybe you have to go through the training regime yourself to really understand. Soon I was back to normal and in a good mood – such a good mood, in fact, that in the hotel room me and Manos started to wrestle each other for fun. That little tussle cost us dear, though – Manos managed to somehow cut my leg so it started to bleed. It wasn't a big wound but it was still a wound. If you get a cut just before a fight then you can't carry on. We'd been there before, so Manos and I got pretty anxious.

Right then there was a knock on the door. I opened it and it was Claes from Unibet.

'Everything alright?' he said.

'Err . . . yeah,' I said. 'But do you have any alcohol I could clean this with?'

I pointed to the cut and went into the bathroom to look in the mirror.

Thankfully it wasn't a big deal in the end, but I saw an opportunity to have some fun with Andreas. I went back out to where Manos and Claes were and picked up the phone. Andreas answered almost straight away.

'I'm cut!'

It was deathly silent at the other end.

'You must be fucking kidding me!'

'No, I'm not.'

It went quiet again, but I couldn't stop myself from cracking up.

'You dick!' shouted Andreas. 'You absolute dick!'

Later that evening me and Manos watched a film. Because the fight was going to start so late the next day, it was important I didn't go to sleep too early. Watching films is also a great way to pass the time if you want to distract yourself. The worst thing you can do is think too much about the fight in your head, or at least it is twenty-four hours before you actually get in the ring.

The following day me, my coach, Jimmy and Manos were collected from the hotel by UFC at eight in the evening and taken to the arena. There was still a lot of time to wait before the fight and my nerves were starting to get to me.

After an hour or so, Big John McCarthy, who would ref the fight, came into the changing room to give us a rundown.

'During the fight, I don't care how you defend yourself, as long as you defend yourself, OK?'

Then Stitch came in to do my hands. Jacob 'Stitch' Duran is a cutman, meaning he has to sew up what he can during the fight if you get injured, stop any bleeding and keep the swelling down. He's also the one who rubs our faces with Vaseline before a fight, the idea being that you don't pick up cuts from being clipped. It still happens, but it reduces the risk as the other guy's hand slides straight over your cheek. Every cutman has his own way of working and treating fighters, and I had specifically asked for Stitch for the fight. My reasoning was simply that he was a great guy.

Finally it was time. Just as people have always asked me why I took The Mauler as my ring name, they also ask me why I choose to come out to a particular song. The truth is there is no deep thinking behind it. The Mauler was a name I was given way back, and I tend to choose the songs depending on what feels right at the time. Whatever I end up choosing I always get butterflies in my stomach as it kicks in. I'm not scared of pain or getting injured, but I am scared of making mistakes and losing. That night I had chosen Avicii's 'Wake Me Up', booming from the loudspeakers. But all I remember from the walkout is that I was running through my tactics and game plan in my head like crazy.

This was Jones, so naturally there was more pressure than usual. Everything was bigger: the arena, the crowd, the lights, everything. Once Stitch had put Vaseline on my face and I had my gumshield in, I climbed into the Octagon. *This is it,* I thought.

Andreas gave me a slap on the shoulder and tried to get me going. 'Let's go,' he shouted, but I could see a nervous expression in his eyes that wasn't normal for him.

'No problem,' I ventured back and shrugged my shoulders. It didn't seem to have much of an effect on either him or me. However I looked at it, I had built a monster in my head. I tried not to stress, but it ground away in my brain: *This is the best fighter ever. He has beaten everyone I have ever admired.*

My memory is sketchy about what happened in the time it took Jones to reach the Octagon. Suddenly he was there and I heard through a haze, 'If you wanna touch gloves then touch 'em now . . . step back . . . good luck to both of you.'

My temples were pounding in time with my heart.

I tried to get a feel for him; distance, his reach and his tactics. What would he do, and how would he attack?

He tried a kick and gave me a punch. It didn't hurt, or at least not as much as I thought it would.

I started working at him, always moving. I didn't let him out of my sight and managed to glance him. I didn't feel it and only noticed when I heard Andreas shouting, 'He's cut, he's cut!' Blood was coming from his eyebrow.

That was it – the noise of the crowd came back into my ears and the monster I had built up in my head was destroyed. *I can do this*, I thought.

Jones's kicks and punches were not as hard as I had expected, but I was also surprised he wasn't better at taking people down. When I managed to take *him* down at the end of the first round I thought something must be wrong. It shouldn't have been that easy – Jones had never been taken down before. That's part of the fun of MMA: you never know what it is like to fight someone until you do it. In Jones's case I was also quite sure he had underestimated me as much as I had built him up into some kind of hero. With the first round done, I knew I had won it. All he had to show for it was an elbow in the final few seconds.

In the second round I went at him with the same tactics as in the first and managed to grab one of his kicks and take him down again. Because I'd already cut his eyebrow, I knew he was sensitive there and tried to work him methodically. Jones tried to do everything he could to take me down, without success. It must have been frustrating for him, and when the second round came to an end I knew I had won it as well.

His only real weapon was his kicks, which he aimed at my body before swinging up towards my head. In round three I noticed he had changed tactics, presumably because he knew he was trailing. Andreas screamed at me to keep my hands high, but the longer you fight the more tired you get. Sometimes things are easier said than done. I had a lot of energy at any rate, and I gave Jones a left-hander, a right-hander and an uppercut. The only effective thing he had to throw at me were his inside-leg kicks, but I got in more blows than he did and managed to injure him more than he could injure me. When round three was over I instinctively felt I had won that one as well.

In the sixty seconds before round four kicked off, Andreas spoke to me.

'You have to be on your toes. Jones is beginning to feel inferior. He'll try something. He'll have an ace up his sleeve.'

Even in round four things went alright, though. I felt agile and could feel myself pulling him apart. I pushed on and landed a whole load of punches. Jones meanwhile was still trying to get me on the floor and failing. Only towards the end of the round did he manage to get me with a spinning elbow after a few attempts. If you know the impact is coming then it is easier to take, because you tense your muscles at the same time as it hits you. But this came out of nowhere and my vision went black. It was like my legs vanished. For the rest of the fight I could see three Joneses dancing around me in the cage.

Giving up was not an option. I had the points advantage and the only way for Jones to win was to finish me completely. And he couldn't. On the other hand he did manage to take me down once more in round five, but I got up again. We traded blows, and when he tried another spinning elbow he got one in return. I could see him glancing at the clock, a sign of weakness and a signal your opponent is feeling tired, or maybe wants out for another reason. Soon after that I got him straight in the mouth, and for the final few minutes he didn't look all there. I knew he had to finish me properly to win and he couldn't make it happen. When the fifth round came to an end, I hoped they would call out my name when the scores were given. The thing was, I knew it was too even to take the belt off him. I had given my all, but it wasn't enough.

Later on I found out that a lot of people had questioned the judges' decision just as much as I had. Phil Davis had run up to Unibet Claes straight after the fight, shouting, 'We won, we won!' The American TV commentators meanwhile had openly declared me to be the winner on points. In the Hilton bar that night the fight was a hot topic. People were pissed off I hadn't got the victory. But I didn't hear any of this until the next day, because right then I was sat in the changing room feeling pretty fragile. Simply getting up hurt, not because Jones had hit me, but because I had driven my body into the ground. I was like an orange that had been squeezed dry. Only the skin was left. I was mentally destroyed, too. I had spent years struggling to make that fight happen and it was all over.

Still, Jones came off a lot worse than I did. He couldn't walk on his own and was helped from the arena to be taken straight to hospital. I ended up there as well to get a cut in my head seen to and for a routine check-up. It meant neither of us made it to the obligatory press conference after.

As I mentioned, Mum always hates it when I have to fight. However, she always wants to be in the arena praying for me, and I am always thankful for it. Even if I can't see her in the stands, I can feel she is there. She had watched all of my fight with Jones (or rather, shut her eyes and peeked through her fingers) together with her new partner, Jarmo. They came to see me at the hospital with Anna, but apparently the first person they laid eyes on was Jones. He was in a hospital bed completely smashed to bits. Mum said she gave him a death stare. She found me a little further on behind a curtain, so full of adrenalin I was shaking. I didn't think it was too bad myself. They'd stitched up my head and patched me up, but Mum still broke down in tears when she saw me.

'Mum, take it easy, take it easy,' I said.

Eventually she calmed down, but when we were all ready to leave again she couldn't help but throw Jones another stern look.

The following day me, Jimmy, Manos, Anna and Claes all sat down to watch the fight on a laptop in Manos's hotel room. I stopped after the first round. I was still too upset by the points call to watch any more.

Instead I took myself off to the CN Tower, the highest building in Toronto. My whole body hurt like hell, not least my legs. I was also pissing blood, and would do so for a couple of days.

When we were done we left for the airport in good time. Claes must have felt sorry for me, because he went straight to the desk and tried to get me an upgrade. UFC are frugal, diplomatically put, and always book economy tickets for their fighters. You don't even get enough passes to your own events for your whole team to come. My Mum, sisters, girlfriend and friends always have to buy their own at full price. The girl at the desk said she would see what she could do about an upgrade and disappeared. There was about half an hour left before the check-in closed, but after fifteen minutes she was still not back. We wondered what had happened and Claes started talking to the girl at the next counter. She said the girl we were dealing with would definitely be back soon. Another ten minutes passed and Claes tried again.

'Excuse me,' he said, 'but we really need to check in now, this is our flight. You have to help us.'

The girl at the next counter just looked at him.

'She'll be back soon to help you,' she muttered and carried on nonchalantly ignoring us.

Time passed and soon the check-in was closed. Only then did the girl at our desk return.

'What do we do now?' said Claes.

The girl shrugged her shoulders.

'Uh, well check-in is now closed,' she said.

I went and sat on a bench across the hall. I could not be bothered taking this one. The guys stayed where they were and carried on arguing with the girl. After a while they came over and gestured towards a counter across the terminal building that we had to go to. I followed them over, but behind the other counter was a man who seemed equally uninterested in helping us. Claes explained the situation.

'Oh, well I'm not sure what I am supposed to do about that.'

It was a really fucking difficult situation, bluntly put.

The man behind the counter made a phone call and started to speak to someone.

Fifteen minutes later he was still speaking, counting some notes and coins in his hand at the same time. Soon enough another half hour had passed and we were running out of time to catch the next flight, too. Suddenly he put down the phone and looked up at us.

'Good news. You can take the London flight!'

Chapter 16

MMA Explodes

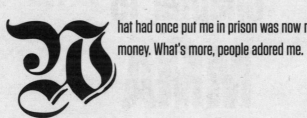hat had once put me in prison was now making me money. What's more, people adored me.

Suddenly everyone knew who I was; suits, builders, kids, teenagers, and even old women who would come up wanting an autograph and a selfie. Even though I never got into this game for the fame, I still thought it was pretty cool. Well, cool was perhaps an over-statement. When the tenth person in a row had come over to chat while I was trying to eat dinner at a restaurant with my mates, it could get tiresome. But it was still recognition of my achievements and Mum felt the same. What had once put me in prison was now making me money. What's more, people adored me.

Mum always said I was a born fighter, that it was my gift – fighting. It seemed to come as a relief to her that I had turned myself around and channelled it into something good. Instead of illegal street fighting we could go at each other in the cage. Half of all cage fighters might have a normal background and some kind of education, but there are quite as many who have been saved by the sport, like I was. Throughout my career I've met guys who have spent their whole lives being told how bad they are. The moment they set foot in an MMA gym, they realise it isn't true. They can fight, and the sport gives them a feeling of purpose as well as making sure they're not throwing punches on the streets.

From a situation where nobody in Sweden gave MMA the time of day, we had reached a point where the big Swedish papers *Expressen* and *Aftonbladet* were going to start covering it seriously. When I came back from America, every morning TV show wanted me on their sofa. Even the sports report on public TV showed footage from the fight.

I may have lost on points, but a lot of people were on my side and thought I had actually won the fight. A lot of people in the MMA world were openly questioning the decision, and the footballer Zlatan Ibrahimovic tweeted: 'For me you were the clear winner.' Me and Zlatan don't know each other and have never met, but I respect him for his sporting achievements and the tweet cheered me up, as did the general praise and words of encouragement everyone seemed to be giving me.

At the same time as all this was happening, something had begun to affect me. A year or so later it would take me to a very dark place, but right then I wasn't really conscious of it, because like so many others I was hoping for a rematch. I also wondered what I would do with the tattoo on my right shoulder. Until then I'd had a shark's tooth inked for every victory and an empty tooth for my defeat to Phil Davis. After the Jones fight I didn't get anything done. Only a while later did I get half a tooth inked, simply because it felt wrong to leave it completely empty.

Usually I rest for a few weeks after a fight. This time it took much longer than usual before I could get back in the gym. Instead I found myself on endless marketing trips with Manos, including to the Philippines, Singapore and Indonesia. It was crazy, especially the Philippines. We were collected by limo at the airport in Manila, or rather by three limos to carry the promoters, me, Manos and six Filipino bodyguards. On the way to the hotel I was dying for a cup of coffee and asked if we could stop. Suddenly all three cars turned around and drove me to a 7-Eleven. Then one of the bodyguards went in to buy the coffee, and when me and Manos were shown to our rooms they waited outside the door with guns. We both thought it was a bit much, but what we said made no difference. If I needed anything, one of them would go and get it for me. To go out on my own was out of the question. Sure, Manila might be a dangerous town with knife fights and the rest, but this was ridiculous.

One of the first things in the diary when I woke up with terrible jet-lag the following morning was a public training session in a big shopping centre, followed by a signing. I didn't really know what to expect. I had never been to the country before, so I was surprised to say the least when I came out on stage on the ground floor of the mall to be met by 4,000 cheering Filipino fans. When I was done and was getting changed for the signing, I saw a boy push through the crowd and grab one of my sweaty socks. After a few days of similar events with my bodyguards in tow I began to get bored. One afternoon, when me and Manos were on our way down from the hotel room, I grabbed the pistol from our door guard's holster and pointed it at Manos. The bodyguard just laughed.

Manos, on the other hand, turned pale.

'Give that back,' he gasped.

I didn't, of course. Instead I pointed it at his head.

Manos looked like he was about to shit himself. I kept up the pretence to see his reaction, but eventually gave the gun back to its owner.

That evening Manos fell ill. He almost always ends up ill or horrendously sunburned when we go abroad. This time around he gave the toilet his full attention for twenty-four hours, so the final few events in Manila were me on my own. Well, not quite alone; I still had my bodyguards.

When me and Manos got back to Sweden there was talk of a rematch against Jones, but it was only talk. I needed another fight before I could get back in the ring with him, which is to say I had to win my next fight and he had to win his. I think he must have been grateful for the break. Of all the fighters he could meet in the light-heavyweight group, I was the worst possible for him. Instead he had been given a clash against Glover Teixeria and I was going to fight Little Nog in London. Me and Little Nog were supposed to have met at the Stockholm Globe back in 2012, but like the first time he ended up picking up an injury before the event.

As a replacement, I was told at the start of November I would be facing Jimi 'Poster Boy' Manuwa.

For the last fight I had prepped at Alliance in San Diego, but this time round we decided to do the whole thing at Allstars in Stockholm. The problem was, with so many journalists trying to get hold of me for five minutes to talk about my next fight, I found it hard to train in peace. I also have my own routines before each fight and it was hard to make stuff work as long as I was at home.

When I got back at night Anna and the dogs were there, and everything was just cosy.

To keep myself motivated, and to keep the fire under my feet, I have to be forced out of my comfort zone in training and into choppier waters. Put more bluntly, I need to have the shit beaten out of me in each and every session. Manos, Andreas and Tomas helped me to find streetfighters from all over the world, and eventually they had a bus load: two Romanians, fifteen Poles, two Finns and a Dutch guy. Now every single day was a full-on assault.

Over Christmas and New Year 2013 we had a little break in training. As usual I was going to celebrate with Mum, my sisters, and Grandma in Sörby. My biological father had been living in Borås, near Gothenburg, for a few years and I hadn't seen him, but I'd been pushing him to come up and see us in Sörby for New Year. In the end he actually caved in and showed.

It felt good to have us all together for once, even though Dad was in a bad way. After he had run off to Thailand years before, it turned out that he had contracted TB and they'd had to take out one of his lungs. He had also drunk his way to a diabetes diagnosis, and was over six feet tall but weighed only 65 kilos. However, you could see his eyes light up when he arrived. I think he was really happy we were all doing alright.

When he left I had a strong feeling it would be our last encounter. Our New Year at Sörby was a kind of farewell. As it turned out, I was right. Soon after he went home to Borås he went hyperglycemic in his sleep and never woke up.

The funeral was held in Arboga. Even though Dad had lived most of his adult life in the north and in Borås, it was there in Västmanland he belonged. I carried the urn and the whole ceremony was beautiful. The trouble was, it felt like I had no chance to really grieve or work through what had happened. I was in the middle of my fight prep and the fight itself was getting closer. I also had a load of other stuff to deal with. In a new campaign called *What'll it be?* I was one of a load of well-known faces who were going to help kids choose the right college courses. The fight between me and Jones was also voted bout of the year at the MMA awards in Las Vegas. I was picked out as Fighter of the Year at the same event. They wanted me to go over and collect the prizes in person, but Tomas and Manos fixed it so I didn't have to.

Another thing in my schedule was a new PS4 and Xbox MMA game from EA Sports. There had been an internet vote to decide who got to stand next to Jones on the cover. Eleven million people had taken part, a huge majority backing me for the picture. It was amazing, but because so much was going on and I had to focus on the training, I didn't have time to take it all in.

Finally we got to 8 March and it was time for UFC Fight Night 37, where I would face Manuwa. TV4 Sport and C More Extreme were broadcasting it live in Sweden, and the newspaper *Dagens Nyheter* published an eight-page piece about it. The sports programme on public TV also did a segment, and they even did a version for kids.

Every single seat at the O2 Arena in London was taken. Fifteen thousand people. There were three thousand Swedes there, and when I walked in to Max Martin's modern version of the Swedish national anthem the noise was deafening. I did everything to ignore it, but sometimes you just can't. A win against Manuwa meant a rematch against Jones, and another opportunity to get hold of the title belt. Fittingly, Manuwa tried the same staredown tactic Jones had by not looking me in the eye. Less than a minute in, though, I knew it was all OK. He was too slow and soon enough I had him on the floor. It was all part of my game plan; I might be quicker than Manuwa, but he kicks like a horse. Those muscular kicks use up a whole lot of oxygen, so I spent the first part of the fight doing all I could to tire him out.

In the second round I got a finger into his eye and he called in the doctor. As I jumped on the spot to stop myself seizing up, I heard him say, 'I can see two of him.' At the same time Andreas shouted, 'He wants out, finish him!'

Andreas was right, because calling on the doctor is a last resort. After that anything can happen. Whether you've taken one in the balls or been jabbed in the eye, you claim everything is fine and carry on, even if it is serious. You do it because you want to win. If you want out, however, it can all be over very quickly, and that was what happened with Manuwa. When the ref got the match going again I got a knee in, missed an uppercut and tried another, then followed up with a flurry of punches and finished him on a TKO.

Anyone watching the fight could see how happy and relieved I was. It was like everything had been lifted from my shoulders.

My coach and my training partner (Ilir Ilifi, who had also won his fight that night) ran over to me. In the stands the Swedish fans waved signs Unibet had handed out. On one side they said *Go Alex!* and on the other *Jones you're next!*

Chapter 17
Waiting for the Rematch

e and Manos sat in the Jacuzzi with a load of naked Arab guys, and before we went to bed the Prince insisted I point my finger at a picture of Jones.

After London I had planned to take a holiday with Grandma to Israel. Unfortunately Grandma had to cancel as she was booked in for a hip operation. Instead I ended up going away again on another UFC marketing trip.

On these sort of trips there is often a big gang of you, so it reminds me of the TV show *Entourage*. We are basically a group of mates, who work together first and foremost because we are mates. On 6 April 2014 we flew to the UAE, where we were going to meet sponsors, say hi to the fans and do interviews. I was also a guest fighter at UFC Fight Night 39 in Abu Dhabi.

It was me, Andreas, Majdi, the co-owner of Allstars, as well as Gabbe, my training coordinator (another co-owner and responsible for arranging all our parties) and Manos.

UFC had booked a room for us at the Crown Plaza on Yas Island, outside Abu Dhabi. The city was the location for most of the marketing stuff and the interviews, but it is not the most fun city in the world. That is especially true at night, so Manos had booked a last-minute room for us at the Mövenpick Hotel in Dubai. That was where we checked in first – the double room was by no means big and there were five of us, but somehow we all squeezed in. Even so, the competition for the bathroom was intense.

One advantage of prepping for a fight is being able to eat whatever the hell you like. When we got up the next day this insane breakfast buffet awaited us. Then it was time for me and Manos to go off to The Westin hotel in Al Sufouh to meet a group of local journalists. They got twenty minutes each and it was a bit of a conveyor belt.

After that I did a TV interview with the Dubai One channel in Media City, before going back to the hotel. Gabbe, assigned with making sure we have a good time on these trips, listed the options for that evening, all of which were clubs with our names on the guest list. Only Gabbe was really keen on hitting the town, but after a while he managed to win us over against all the odds.

On each trip there tends to be one tune we play to death. This time around it was 'I Follow Rivers' by Lykke Li. Whilst the rest of us got ready and chugged down some drinks, Gabbe played it on loop. As an elite athlete you don't get too many chances to drink, but this was a few weeks after one fight and months before another one. So I took my chance.

The Tuesday was media day in Abu Dhabi at our other hotel, the Crown Plaza. We hadn't slept much, but even so I wasn't all that tired. Not yet at least. Manos was, on the other hand, and our taxi driver even more so. Now and again he would nod off and the car would veer into oncoming traffic. I remember freezing as it happened. We were doing eighty on a road with cars coming the other way and the guy looked like he would go out like a light at any moment!

I told Manos to be ready to grab the wheel if anything happened, as he was sat in the front seat. The problem was that Manos was so sleepy, he only mumbled and dozed off again. Finally we got there in one piece and Vicky, the PR for UFC, showed us in to a small room at the hotel. It was hot, the air con had broken, and I had a load of phone interviews with the US to do. Everyone asked me about Jones's next fight, so I said that Teixeira packed a punch but Jones was a better fighter and would take him without too many problems. They also asked me how I felt about the rematch; did I think Jones was afraid of me? I didn't, but I said I was pretty sure I had got under his skin.

Like the day before, the whole thing was like a conveyor belt. I started to feel as if I was a bird in a cage. My dreams of winning a UFC title had not involved any of this stuff. Outside the MMA scene nobody had cared when I started out, but now every day was a circus.

The PR smiled at me and dialled another number.

This particular journalist talked mostly about my fight with Manuwa. He congratulated me on the victory and asked me how it had felt. I told him it was great to show I was the best in Europe.

Then he started asking about Jones again. I said I'd be better prepared when we next met, and that I would push my body to new extremes so I could finish him in round three or four.

Just like all journalists that wasn't enough for him. He started asking about my future, but I gave the same honest answer as always: I only ever think about my next challenge, my next fight.

In the afternoon I was due to go to a local jiu-jitsu club in Abu Dhabi to get my picture taken with their members.

The place was in the basement of a fairly small apartment block. The only way in was with a slightly rickety lift and the club itself was tiny, more like a room. The guys inside all seemed happy to see me, if a little shy to begin with. At one end of the room was a table for me to sit down at. The guys formed an orderly line and came forward one by one to get a picture with me. Then each of them took my hand in turn and thanked me for coming.

The week carried on in much the same way, by which I mean interviews and PR events. That Thursday me and two other guest fighters – Luke Barnatt and Urijah Faber – did a Q&A on the beach.

Then it was time for the event itself. We got there in time for the main card, luckily as it turned out, because all the fights up to then had apparently been terrible. The main fights were equally bad, but this was my job: I sat in the seat UFC had given me and waved to the cameras when they zoomed in.

After the event we had a bit more fun. I bumped into Manuwa, who I hadn't seen since our London fight. I knew he wanted to come up and train with us at Allstars, so we talked about making it happen. After the post-fight press conference, where I answered identical questions to the ones I had answered all week, Manu said that the Prince of Abu Dhabi had invited us to a party at his private island. Not long after, we were in a boat together with the Prince and his friends.

The journey took about half an hour, and when we arrived me and Manos were given a private bungalow with a personal bartender. It was quite a heavy night, all said, and I can't honestly tell you exactly what happened. What I do remember is that me and Manos sat in the Jacuzzi with a load of naked Arab guys, and before we went to bed the Prince insisted I point my finger at a picture of Jones. Why, I have no idea, but he really insisted on it and because he was a nice guy I did as he asked.

The morning after, we had this mad lobster breakfast and drove about on jet skis. One of the Prince's staff gave us a lift back to the mainland, but not before Manos and the Prince had exchanged phone numbers.

Chapter 18
Bad Boys in Newcastle

ough guys who don't do martial arts just end up in trouble. They get mixed up in bar fights, where the real fighters have nothing to prove. They know they could take anybody.

It was good to be home again, and good to get back to training, even if stuff seemed to always get in the way. I had got a bigger place in Sundbyberg on the north side of town for me, Anna, and the dogs, so we started the move. All the while the number of interviews and PR trips seemed to increase constantly. On 26 April I was due to go to Gothenburg for a showpiece training session to open a new gym. On the 27th, a camera crew from UFC were going to come to my hotel and film me as I watched footage of the Jones–Teixeira fight.

Before the fight Jones had been asked more questions about me and a potential rematch than the man he was about to face off against. I guess it got to him, because he frequently tried to change the subject. He also said he had only given eighty per cent against me the last time, but I didn't care all that much. However, I did have a few issues with what the UFC film crew wanted.

I had just rubbed the sleep from my eyes and put on a top when they knocked on the door. After that, all I could do was play along.

They asked me to go back to bed and pretend to wake up. Then I had to go to the window and look out over Gothenburg. Because I actually had just woken up, we ran through the scene several times until they were happy. Then came the fight. The crew couldn't get it up on Fightpass, UFC's own streaming service, and the minutes ticked by. With time running out, they had no choice but to use a less than legal streaming site.

The idea was that I would comment on what I was watching, so I more or less said what I thought: Jones had done what he needed to do and he was a technical fighter who can adapt to his opponent. I also said I was pleased he won – now I could have my rematch.

The camera crew packed up their stuff, and so did I. I wanted to get back to Stockholm and properly sort our new place after the move.

The only thing was, there was less time than either I or Anna had hoped for. I began to notice things that I had seen with my previous girlfriends; moaning about how much I was away. She was right, of course, because even training at Allstars was a full-time job. Now there was so much else to do as well.

On 11 May I was at the Budo & Fitness event at the Stockholm Globe for one of my sponsors. They had a stand where I would get my photo taken with fans and sign autographs. It wasn't all that taxing in itself, but it took time. I was away from training and away from Anna. What's more, a few days later I was due in England for another sponsor's event.

Every time I leave Stockholm, whether I am going to Mum's for a few nights or travelling abroad, I have to tell the doping commission. They can come to your house and test you without warning, and if you go somewhere without telling anyone, they give you a strike. I had two strikes, and if you get three you are suspended from competition for a year. I hardly need point out what a disaster that would have been in my situation.

I had asked the Martial Arts Federation to deal with all of that for me. Had I done it myself, I would no doubt have had my third strike, partly because I can be careless, but also because I had so much else to think about. It's a pain, but I am a big fan of such tight anti-doping rules. They keep the sport clean, although the problem is that in places like Brazil and the US they are far less stringent. If you face a guy from outside Europe, you can never be quite sure he's not using something.

On 16 May I flew to Newcastle with Manos for an event with Bad Boy, another of my sponsors. It was a dire journey, because we had to fly via Frankfurt and London. We didn't land until fairly late at night.

The next day we had a good hotel breakfast, and for the first time in weeks I felt genuinely relaxed and rested. At ten o'clock the head of Bad Boy, John-Paul, came and drove us to the MetroCentre in Gateshead, where the Bad Boy shop was.

There was already a queue of people outside who wanted my autograph on shirts and photos, both of which you could buy in

Training with Andreas before my fight against Cormier ...

... and exhausted after the workout.

Recording 'Johan Falk', autumn 2014.

Between workouts before the Cormier fight.

This shot was taken right after my title fight in Houston against Cormier, 3 October 2015.

Media day in Houston before my title fight against Cormier.

The day of my book cover photo shoot.

Me and my dog, Ghost.

the shop. I was shown to a table where I got down to work. The whole time I could see the queue just growing and growing. It wasn't until two that me and the boys could get away to eat a cheeky Nandos. Then we went to the Bad Boy gym with John-Paul, which lay in a more run-down part of town.

John-Paul was an ex-con and saw the gym as his way to repay his debt to society. Homeless guys and lads from care homes could train there for free once a week.

John-Paul chatted about it as he drove in to town. 'Tough guys who don't do martial arts just end up in trouble. They get mixed up in bar fights, where the real fighters have nothing to prove. They know they could take anybody.'

I agreed with him, and before we got to the gym we had time to talk about some of the guys training there. A few of them were gym fighters, guys who looked amazing in training but who couldn't cut it in a fight. There were also the opposite, guys who were terrible in prep, but exploded as soon as you put them in a cage. Bad Boy had some of Northern England's best MMA fighters. One of them, Dan Singh, had been in the UK version of *Gladiators* and a good few Hollywood films. Another in their roster was Richie Knox.

My job that afternoon was to hold a training session in the presence of some British combat sports mags, and I think I left them happy. The guys seemed to like having me there, and they were really grateful afterwards.

Because me and Jones had both won our fights, Dana White and UFC decided it was time for a rematch. It felt fantastic, but Jones refused to sign the contract. He babbled on in the media about how he wanted to face Daniel Cormier instead, but even if Cormier was perhaps a better match for him than I was, I think it was really tactics from his management to push for better terms. Whatever was behind it, Jones got some bad press because of it. Annoyingly for me, it also meant that UFC couldn't fix a date and location for the fight.

When I went to Berlin on 31 May for UFC Fight Night 41 as a guest fighter, as well as to support my Allstars buddies Nicklas Bäckström and Magnus 'Jycken' Cedenblad, I still had no idea when we would be in the ring. Even in June when me, Anna and Manos went away to Manos's holiday place in Greece, we were still in the dark.

It wasn't until late at night on 4 July that I finally found out the date. We were going to fight on 27 September at UFC 178. In Vegas.

Chapter 19
Injury

The only good thing that summer was the seven puppies Sativa gave us.

As an MMA fighter something somewhere always hurts. It needn't be anything serious, but you are basically never injury-free. That was why I didn't think too much about how stiff my knee felt when I got down to fight-prep at Allstars. Sure, I knew I would have to get my meniscus seen to (it is the most common injury from wear and tear amongst elite athletes), but I thought I could wait a while longer. I ploughed on as I had been doing, until it suddenly went in a training session on 23 July. The knee just locked and I had to go straight to hospital with Andreas.

Apart from the meniscus there was also a damaged ligament in the knee. The doctor who examined me said he really had no choice but to operate on it, and it knocked me for six. I realised straight away that my prep was as good as over. You don't get in a ring with Jones unless you are in peak condition. All we could do was get Tomas and Manos to contact UFC and cancel the fight. A few days later Jones ended up with the opponent he had always wanted, Daniel Cormier.

Looking back on it now, I can see that the injury was one of a whole load of things that would end badly. It really started when I was told I had to fight Manuwa if I wanted another crack at Jones, but at the time I had no real perspective on the situation. I was so mentally fixed on going up against Jones that thinking anything else was almost impossible.

It didn't help that Jones revealed he would have to delay his fight with Cormier to undergo the same operation that I had. I'd started my rehab by then, so me and my managers thought it was obvious I could fight Jones when he was fully recovered. Nobody could claim I hadn't earned it, but UFC had started to get the machine whirring before the fight, and Jones and Cormier had already started trash-talking one another. We soon realised that it made no difference what we thought.

You also have to remember that there is a lot of politics and business behind it all, and my team tried some hard-nosed negotiation by saying they would wait for the title fight anyway. That didn't work either, so in the end we had no choice but to take another fight before we could get the rematch. Who I would face was the big question.

When I did my first training session after the operation, you could say my motivation wasn't the highest it has ever been. With no fight in sight it can be difficult to keep yourself going. It was made worse by the fact I felt I had been deprived of my rematch twice.

The only good thing that summer was the seven puppies my dog Sativa gave us, and Anna took care of them as I pushed hard at my rehab. There was also a lot of other stuff going on that sent my head in different directions. Towards the end of the summer I was supposed to have a role as an extra in one of the Johan Falk Swedish police films. I had said yes because I had seen all the previous ones myself and liked them, but I also did it because I wanted a challenge. To be honest, I was terrified when I had to record my one little scene, even though I only had to say a single line. When I arrived at the offices of the production company in Hägersten in Stockholm to meet the crew, it felt like my first steps into the lobby of Gladius nearly a decade before.

In the film I was going to play one of the cops in a swat team, so the first thing they did was fit me out with a costume. Then me and Jakob Eklund, who plays Johan Falk, and some of the other actors drove to a house nearby that would stand in for a suburb of Gothenburg.

When we got to the white single-storey house, there were three film trucks outside and all the windows in the building were covered in black plastic. I had absolutely no experience of either acting or filming, but never did I imagine such a tiny little scene could take so long. The first thing we did when everyone was on location was to rehearse the scene, which involved me and some other cops storming the house. I was supposed to shout 'Police!' and take down the villain who was hiding inside. Funnily enough he was being played by a mate of mine, the Allstars coach, Samir Chattay.

We ran through it several times and they had to check the sound, lights, camera angles and everything else. The scriptwriter was a former policeman and followed the director round to make sure everything looked the way it should. At long last we were allowed to start filming. I don't know how many takes it took, but it was all great fun. I got a real kick out of it, and at the end of the day everyone seemed happy with it.

Next day I was back in the gym, but I can't say I was any more excited about it than before. I had recovered from the operation just fine, but I wasn't enjoying it any more. When UFC Fight Night 53 rolled around at the Stockholm Globe on 4 October I still didn't have an opponent lined up. Even so, I still did a load of media stuff and took part in the press conference at the Globe in the run up to the event. And I trained and trained. It was more for the media's sake, who had managed to hype the event to unreal proportions. *Aftonbladet* even did a whole supplement – with me on the front – which they called the MMA Bible. When Saturday came around and it was time for several of my mates from Allstars to climb into the ring at the Globe I was naturally there in the stands.

Unfortunately it didn't turn out well for any of them that night. 'Jycken' managed a hard-fought victory on points, and my old training partner Nico Musoke took another narrow win on points. Ilir Latifi got a kick straight to his liver, and you can't easily come back from that. The pain hits you about thirty seconds after impact, at which point you sink to the floor. That was what happened to Ilir, and he lost on a technical knockout to Jan Blachowicz. My buddy Niklas Bäckström got knocked out in the first round against the English fighter Mike Wilkinson. It was a terrible night, not only for the Allstars squad, but for Swedish MMA generally.

Things started to feel pretty hopeless for me, too. At the beginning of November I still had no word about who my next opponent would be. We had ten different names thrown at us, but all of them pulled out. However, Jones and Cormier had a new fixture arranged – if both could stay injury-free they were due to meet in Vegas at UFC 182 on 3 January 2015.

Finally, in the middle of November, I was given an opponent: Anthony 'The Rumble' Johnson. By this point Tomas had written and deleted countless press releases about new fights, but this time everything seemed to be concrete. On 24 January me and Anthony would meet in Stockholm at the Tele2 Arena, which was entirely down to Tomas and Manos. They had been fighting hard for a long time to make sure I would be facing someone on home turf. UFC had doubted whether we could really fill a stadium at four in the morning, because the fight was going out live on US TV, but somehow we managed to convince them.

UFC had also promised us I would get another title fight sometime in the spring if I made sure I emerged victorious from my bout with Anthony. The problem was that almost straight away I went and strained the ligaments in my knee in a training session. Me and Andreas found ourselves back at the hospital, where the doctor ordered me to rest the leg for at least six weeks. What's more, I had to wear a brace on it everywhere except in bed. It wasn't going to work; I needed to get going on my fight camp to make sure I was one hundred per cent ready for the bout. It would also have been a total catastrophe if people got wind of my injury. Anthony would definitely try and use it against me and do whatever he could to kick the bad knee. If UFC found out, then the fight was off, full stop. It was probably the worst thing that could have happened to me, because right then all I wanted to do was move on, at any price. The only thing I could do was leave the leg brace on the shelf at home as we flew to Vegas for the biggest press conference in the history of UFC.

We landed in the early evening on 16 November and were at the hotel by eight. Even though I had done my usual thing and not slept a wink on the flight, I was in no rush to go to bed. Instead we dropped the bags and went to grab some food at a Japanese place in the hotel, then we finished up by going to a club Andreas knew.

The following morning UFC were going to film me in my room as I got ready for the press conference. There was also a Swedish camera crew, who had come to Vegas to make a documentary for the TV4 channel in the run-up to my fight. When the luxury bus picked us up at the hotel at twelve, I had been awake and at it for a fair few hours. It was a right mixture of guys on the bus. Across from me was Jon Jones, and next to him sat Chris Weidman, Anderson Silva and Ronda Rousey. Right at the front you also had Conor McGregor, Nick Diaz and Lyoto Machida.

We were all fairly quiet, chatting politely and making conversation. When we got to the Smith Centre where they were doing the press conference the mood lightened and we paraded up the red carpet, surrounded by fans, photographers and reporters. Once again it was me and Jones who were the centre of attention. They asked us to do some staredowns and we took questions about what we thought of each other's coming fights.

There were fourteen of us at that press conference, which was led by Dana White and attended by a few hundred journalists. It was also broadcast live on the web and on US TV. I was still exhausted from the flight the day before, and concentrated solely on not falling over as I got up to go off behind the scenes and talk to people in interview rooms.

Chapter 20

Anthony 'Rumble' Johnson

The expectation levels were high. They had sold 25,000 tickets and it looked like it would be the best attended UFC event ever.

At the beginning of December we started the training camp. It was as hellish as always before I grew accustomed to the training routine again. I also had a swollen knee to think about, and there were times where I just had to stop. The doctor at the hospital in Stockholm had ordered six weeks of rest, but I thought that if the knee survived the training, it would survive the fight. The real issue was that I couldn't go all in, and that left me frustrated.

Another thing that got to me was all the media circus. It used to be that the interviews were something I could deal with well enough, but I had my own PR officer now who would say yes to everything. Your prep for a fight is mental as well as physical, and it is hard to maintain your focus when there are journalists hanging round the gym. As well as the guys from TV4 there was the UFC crew, and God knows what they were doing.

It all made me feel like a monkey in a cage. To get myself ready for the weird fight in the middle of the night I would soon have to begin sleeping all day and training after dark. For the time being I did two sessions, one at nine in the morning and the other at two in the afternoon.

Because of the knee I couldn't do my usual physical conditioning, so I replaced the sessions with swims at Stockholm's Olympic-size pool.

Thankfully I had some really great partners to spar against. On 12 December I did some old-school exercises with this amazing light-heavyweight boxer from Kyrgyzstan. It was stuff like smashing a ball as hard as you could at a wall and imagining it had passed right through, and lifting weights super quick with your right hand.

The following day was St Lucia's Day and I was looking forward to relaxing at home that weekend with Mum and Grandma in the country. Unfortunately it wasn't to be. Both UFC and the TV4 team came to interview me and the family. On the Monday we got back to training, and once again the gym was packed with journalists. You can't relax when people are there filming and taking photos.

The plan was to try a few different techniques, but I ended up just sparring with some of the other Allstars fighters.

Andreas walked around shouting 'Tempo!' and 'Hands up!' as he usually did at anyone who relaxed or let their guard down. Then we finished the session with crunches, sit-ups, press-ups and some shadow boxing.

Before I left the gym, me and Andreas watched footage of Rumble on Andreas's iPad. Ilir joined us.

'Anthony is like a tortoise,' he said. 'If he is on his back he has no idea how to get up again.'

It would turn out later that Ilir was right, but right then all I felt was frustration at not being able to train and do rehab on my knee in peace and quiet. A few days later me and Andreas decided to leave all that shit behind. Together with a few sparring partners and Jimmy we got on a plane to San Diego and Alliance.

There was lots to like about being in San Diego beyond getting into my training rhythm. The sun helped my rehab and soon enough the knee started to feel good, even though I was far from recovered.

Ten days before the fight we came home to an ice-cold and pitch-black Stockholm. The expectation levels were high. They had sold 25,000 tickets and it looked like it would be the best-attended UFC event ever. Someone had written that never before had a combat sports event in Sweden drawn in such a big crowd, and it might have been true. It was hysterical, but when you are in the middle of it you can't really take it all in. I also had my own stuff to deal with; I had to try and keep my American body clock and do the final few sessions overnight at Allstars. Not only that, but I still had to be available for interviews that could sell even more tickets for the event.

Journalists kept on asking questions about my rematch with Jones rather than the fight I was about to step into the ring for. The papers wrote things like: 'This is the fight that will give Alexander Gustafsson another shot at the title.' The pressure on me had never been greater. I like a challenge and usually thrive on them, but this was beyond comparison. It was like every person on Earth was pulling me in a different direction, and when the weigh-in came around I was feeling ropey and had a fever.

I don't mention it as an excuse for what happened, as the fever was mostly gone the following day, but I didn't feel any pleasure at climbing into the Octagon. Nor did I feel motivated. The fact was (and only then did I realise it) that I had not felt any desire to fight since my meeting with Jones. When it was finally time for me and the team to walk out in front of 27,000 screaming fans at the Tele2, Andreas asked me, 'Aren't you nervous?'

Andreas knows me well, sometimes better than I know myself, and I am always a touch nervous before my fights. But not that day. I don't want to sound uninterested – it was amazing to see that sea of people and hear the booming crowd when I walked out – but I just wasn't there. The next thing I remember is me and Anthony Johnson standing face to face. Somewhere in the distance the ref's voice said, 'Let's do this.'

Then we were away. He landed a few blows and I did the same, and things started to feel good for the most part, even though I was less aggressive than usual. When I poked Johnson in the eye by accident the ref temporarily called a halt and Andreas screamed, 'Front kick!' at me. That's how these things work: my coach screams at me what I should do and sometimes you find a chink in the armour and go for it.

Except then I did it without any real bite. I kicked, but Johnson got hold of my leg and after that there was little I can remember. By that I mean that my final memory of that fight was being on all fours. It felt like I was drowning in quicksand, and all I could think was: *I have to get up before the ref blows for the end of the fight. If I don't get up now I'm finished.*

Soon after it was over anyway, and I was judging myself mercilessly. Andreas rushed into the Octagon and I hugged him. I broke down and began to cry more than I had cried in years. All my friends were there at the Tele2, and so were my relatives and 27,000 others who had come to see me win. It was like I hadn't only let myself and my team down but the entire Swedish nation.

The days after the fight were hazy. What's more, I felt weird in the head. My managers booked me in for a head X-ray, but it showed no sign of injury from Anthony, at least not physically. I did feel mentally destroyed, though. Luckily I had my family and my friends, and they supported me in all kinds of ways.

Jimmy kept trying to persuade me I needed to get away and arranged a trip to Thailand for us and our girlfriends. We really needed it and had a good time out there. For the first time in ages I could leave training and MMA behind me. I think me and the team were all hoping those two weeks would give me back my thirst to compete. As soon as I was back in Sweden, however, I fell into the rut again and didn't even want to set foot in the gym. It stressed me out; for so long MMA had been part of my identity that I didn't know who I was without it. All the same, there was nothing to make me go back to it. Thoughts raced around my head. Most of all I began to think about my future. What the hell would I do? Take a normal job? Everything felt as possible as it did impossible. Before the fight against Johnson I had bought a place in the country with a lot of land attached. Should I move out there permanently and live on the money I had until it was gone?

For the first time since my teenage years I was totally lost. My managers did what they could to help me, and eventually I agreed to see a sports psychologist at their suggestion. But when I got back into the gym I was no happier, which is to say that I arrived angry and left angry.

Soon UFC got in touch to tell me they had another opponent for me, Glover Teixeira, and they wanted us to fight that spring in Berlin. My coaches and managers were totally against the idea. They reckoned

I needed to rediscover my enthusiasm for the sport and build up my body again in peace and quiet. I told them I was up for the fight; I thought if only I could get a new fight the motivation and the enthusiasm would come back again. What they said made no difference and I had stopped listening. I just wanted to move on.

After a while they started to see things my way, but the prospect of facing Teixeira didn't make me any more cheerful. I only went to the gym sporadically, and when I was there I hardly spoke to anyone. If I did I was either annoyed or angry. At the same time me and Anna fell apart. I couldn't do it any more. Everything was such a fucking struggle. I was also having some issues with my back, but that was not the reason I rang Tomas and told him to cancel the fight.

Tomas did not even sound surprised, but for me the conversation was an enormous relief. There then followed long chats with Tomas, Manos and Andreas. Soon we were agreed that we would go back to their original plan. Slowly but surely we would build my strength up and take a fight when we were ready, with whoever it was, in the autumn.

In one of the hunting shops where I used to buy my kit there was this really nice blonde girl called Moa, who I had started chatting to. To begin with we talked about hunting, but after a while it became a bit more general. We talked about exercise and training, because she was always in the gym herself, so I invited her down to Allstars. A few days later she came by, so I showed her around and we did a session together. When we were done I gave her a lift home, and could immediately feel that I liked her drive. This was a girl who wanted something from life. We started dating and soon we had moved in and decided to try having a serious relationship.

It was around then I heard the news that Jon Jones had been arrested after a hit-and-run incident and he'd had his title belt taken off him. He was also banned from UFC for an indefinite period. It was his second scandal in a short space of time, and I felt a bit sorry for him. At the same time I knew UFC had done the right thing. You have a certain responsibility towards the young boys and girls who look up to you when you are at this level. Pound for pound Jones was the best fighter in UFC, and he had thrown it all away because of the crash. It was hard for me, too, because I had fought for so long to get my rematch. Even if it wasn't happening straight away, there was still the prospect it might happen. Instead they had fixed it so that Anthony Johnson and Daniel Cormier would fight for the title, and Tomas was enthusiastic when I went down to the gym a few days later.

'Cormier will take it,' he said.

I don't remember what I said, but I was hardly as convinced of the outcome as he was.

'Cormier will push him up against the edge of the cage and strangle him.'

Tomas was right. At UFC 187 on 23 May Cormier beat Anthony Johnson in the third round. By then I had started a proper routine back at the gym and was slowly but surely finding my way back to form. One day, the week after Cormier's victory, Tomas came up to me after my afternoon session and said a title fight between me and Cormier might be on the cards.

'Get away,' I said.

'It's your turn though.'

'Never, I'm coming straight out of a defeat.'

But Tomas insisted. He really believed I was in a position to fight for the title, and when we left each other I was feeling quite annoyed with him.

A week later he called my mobile. We speak almost every day anyway, but that day there was something in his voice that told me it was different.

'What did I tell you?'

'When?'

'When we spoke to each other after Cormier beat Johnson.'

I was in the car on the way to the gym.

'You've got a title fight. UFC want you to face Cormier in the autumn.'

Chapter 21
For the Win

everal times when I landed a blow I could see the whites of his eyes. Then he changed gear and suddenly he was like a jeep that had turned on the four-wheel drive.

The plan was for us to fight in Vegas in September 2015, but because Cormier needed time to recover from an injured knee, they had put it back a month and changed the location to Houston. At long last I was sat in the changing room at a sold-out Toyota Center, shared with Rashad Evans. My prep had gone well and although a lot was at stake I felt calm and collected. Me and Andreas had got to the arena a few hours before the fight, and once we had said hi to Rashad and his coaches I started to warm up.

It is vital to get your heart rate up and give yourself a bit of a sweat so you don't get a shock when you step in. We did our usual drills with a bit of wrestling, a bit of grappling and some step-ups. Everything felt good. Time raced by and the fights on the TV screens in the changing room rolled by in succession. Soon it was my time to go out, and I walked out to the training-montage tune from *Rocky IV.* All the way into the arena I stayed calm, and nothing changed when the fight got going.

Me and the coaches had studied Cormier carefully, but, as I have already said, you don't know what a fighter is like until you meet him in the ring. One of the things that got me about Cormier was his unprecedented strength. There was a moment in the fight when he lifted me as if I weighed nothing, put me on the floor and started working away at me. I quickly realised it would be a problem. It was all so quick, and I thought how bad things looked for me. I would have to get up on my feet again. You can never forget that the fight is mental, too, and the guy who takes down his opponent first automatically takes control. On top of that, defending yourself on your back takes a lot of effort. I was getting tired, but managed to pull myself up and finish the round on my feet.

As the fight went on I was struck by the feeling that there was no chance of me knocking this guy out. In the second round I had him on the floor and hit him with everything I could muster – knees, kicks and everything else – but he just carried on. I have floored people left, right and centre in fights and training, but he just pushed and pushed. We ended up in a clinch several times, and though the hits I took weren't powerful, they did a lot of damage. At one point I lost vision in my right eye and thought the cornea had torn.

In the break Andreas, Ilir and the others gave me instructions. I can't remember exactly what they said, only that Andreas basically told me to work harder and the fight would be mine.

The third round went much the same as the first two. I hit him in the stomach a fair bit and could hear that I'd winded him. Still he carried on. How on earth was I supposed to stop this guy? I glanced over at my coaches a few times, but I couldn't hear them because the crowd were making so much noise. Maybe I should have tried a few more things myself, but I didn't. I threw myself at him, overcome with tiredness. I could feel a desperation creeping in. I was making no progress. Towards the end of the third round I finally managed to get him with a knee to the head and followed up with a left hook that put him on the floor. This was it, I felt. But somehow he managed to get up again and survive until the end of the round.

Round four was like walking on quicksand. Several times when I landed a blow I could see the whites of his eyes. Then he changed gear and suddenly he was like a jeep that had turned on the four-wheel drive. I knew what it was like to fight for a points victory against a champion in his home turf. I knew what might happen. It was making me agitated, and the agitation began to tire me out.

The fight got tougher and tougher, and by round five I was thinking it was about survival now. It was a fight where the final round came to strength of will from both sides. There was one blow I took from him when I thought to myself *shit, that was big*, but the worst thing was the way he ground me down. I couldn't keep him at bay, and he went for my face again and again. By the end of the final round I could feel blood in my mouth, and when the fight was over I found I had a huge cut in my mouth. I don't know how it had happened as I had my shield in.

I felt I had done well enough and was just glad it was over, but when the judges had given their verdict and Cormier won on a split decision I couldn't see any positives in it. Moa came with me in the ambulance to the hospital. I wasn't really injured, but I had some heavy cuts to the face. There were forty stitches in total, of which twenty were on my mouth. My face was like mincemeat.

On the flight home the day after, I was awake with pain whilst everyone else was asleep. I could neither eat nor take snuff. The fight was still whirring away in my head. I was so depressed about it all. What did I do now? I couldn't sleep, I just sat there trying to drink from a plastic glass and spilt the contents. I got so angry I threw the fucking thing. People stared at me. I was raging, and the rage bubbled away all the way home.

Those first few days back in Stockholm I did nothing but sit in front of the TV. I could not sleep, I could hardly swallow and I ate through a straw. The stitches in my cheek felt weird and I fiddled with them constantly. It was compulsive, I couldn't leave them alone. That was a tough time. I wanted to stop competing but carry on training. My two most recent fights had seen me take a fair few blows to the head and I started to think about how it would affect me later in life. Would I be fifty years old and unable to remember my way home?

I also felt that I wanted to go back to America with Moa by my side for six months. We would find a gym, train, and give it one final push.

I have always believed that what drives me is the need to win, to be the best at what I do, and to know that other people think I'm the best, too. But everything I do, everything I have around me, is tied to the sport. I feel that if I can't carry on with it – the only thing that ever took me anywhere – I'll lose it all and slide back into the old habits.

That fear is what really drives me.

Acknowledgements

Alexander Gustafsson: I would like thank my family, my team, my coaches, Perra, Carlos, Jimmy, Andreas and all my friends, my girlfriend Moa, and MMA.

Leif Eriksson and Martin Svensson: When we started this project we did not know much about MMA at all, expecting to encounter a brutal reality in every sense. Instead we have spent two years travelling the world and meeting people. Wherever we went, we were received with more warmth and consideration than we have experienced anywhere else. We have also made a great number of new friends.

Thank you to Alex, Tomas Ghassemi, Manos Terzitane, Andreas Michael, Majdi Shammas, Gabriel Yilmaz, Jimmy Eriksson, Elonara Gustafsson, Seija Samuelsson, Elina Gustafsson, Moa Antonia Johansson, Perra, Andreas, Carlos, Claes Bergström (Unibet), John-Paul Gardner (Bad Boy), Andy Dixon (Bad Boy), and all the fighters at the Allstars Training Center, Niklas Lindblad, Bingo Rimér, and UFC.

Selected Titles and Awards

Mixed Martial Arts
Ultimate Fighting Championship
Fight of the Night vs Jon Jones
Cover for EA Sports UFC

ESPN
2013 Fight of the Year

Sherdog
2013 Fight of the Year

MMAFighting.com
2013 Fight of the Year

Foxsports.com
2013 Fight of the Year

Yahoo! Sports.com
2013 Fight of the Year

Amateur Boxing
Swedish gold, heavyweight (Over 91 kg)
2009 Tensta Box Open Heavyweight Tournament, Winner
2009 KP Cup, super heavyweight, Winner

Submission wrestling
Grapplers Paradise 4, −99 kg (−218 lbs), Winner

Result	Record	Opponent	Method	Event	Date	Round	Time	Location
Loss	16–4	Daniel Cormier (USA)	Judges' decision (split)	UFC 192	3 October 2015	5	5:00	Houston, Texas
Loss	16–3	Anthony Johnson (USA)	TKO (punches)	UFC on Fox 14	24 January 2015	1	2:15	Stockholm, Sweden
Win	16–2	Jim Manuwa (UK)	TKO (knee, punches)	UFC Fight Night 37	8 March 2014	2	1:18	London, England
Loss	15–2	Jon Jones (USA)	Judges' decision (unanimous)	UFC 165	21 September 2013	5	5:00	Toronto, Canada
Win	15–1	Mauricio Rua (Brazil)	Judges' decision (unanimous)	UFC on Fox: Henderson vs Diaz	8 December 2012	3	5:00	Seattle, Washington
Win	14–1	Thiago Silva (Brazil)	Judges' decision (unanimous)	UFC Sweden	14 April 2012	3	5:00	Stockholm, Sweden
Win	13–1	Vladimir Matyushenko (Belarus)	TKO (punches)	UFC 141	30 December 2011	1	2:13	Las Vegas, Nevada
Win	12–1	Matt Hamill (USA)	TKO (punches and elbows)	UFC 133	6 August 2011	2	3:34	Philadelphia, Pennsylvania

Result	Record	Opponent	Method	Event	Date	Round	Time	Location
Win	11–1	James Te-Huna (New Zealand)	Submission (rear naked choke)	UFC 127	27 February 2011	1	4:27	Sydney, Australia
Win	10–1	Cyrille Diabaté (France)	Submission (rear naked choke)	UFC 120	16 October 2010	2	2:41	London England
Loss	9–1	Phil Davis (USA)	Submission (anaconda choke)	UFC 112	10 April 2010	1	4:55	Abu Dhabi, UAE
Win	9–0	Jared Hamman (USA)	KO (punches)	UFC 105	14 November 2009	1	0:41	Manchester, England
Win	8–0	Vladimir Shemarov (Ukraine)	KO (punches)	Superior Challenge 3	30 May 2009	1	2:37	Stockholm, Sweden
Win	7–0	Pedro Quetglas (Spain)	TKO (punches)	The Zone FC 3	8 November 2008	1	2:08	Gothenburg, Sweden
Win	6–0	Krzysztof Kulak (Poland)	Judges' decision (unanimous)	KSW extra	13 September 2008	3	5:00	Dabrowa Górnicza, Poland

Win	5–0	Matteo Minonzio	TKO (punches)	The Zone FC 2	10 May 2008	1	3:52	Gothenburg, Sweden
Win	4–0	Florian Muller (Germany)	TKO (knee to body and punches)	Fite Selektor	13 March 2008	2	3:44	Dubai, UAE
Win	3–0	Farbod Fadami (Germany)	TKO (punches)	The Zone FC 1	9 February 2008	1	2:31	Stockholm, Sweden
Win	2–0	Mikael Haydari (Finland)	TKO (punches)	FinnFight 9	15 December 2007	1	0:50	Turku, Finland
Win	1–0	Saku Heikkola (Finland)	Submission (rear naked choke)	Shooto Finland – Chicago Collision 3	17 November 2007	2	3:42	Lahti, Finland

Swedish MMA Rules

Competition rules for international professional Mixed Martial Arts (MMA), as issued by the Swedish Mixed Martial Arts Association.

1. Event promoter

1.1   The event promoter shall ensure that all laws and regulations are met during the course of the competition.

1.2   The event promoter shall appoint the officials and personnel required for the competition, ensuring that they have appropriate education and experience.

1.3   The event promoter shall apply for sanction for the match no later than three months in advance of the competition date.

1.4   After the conclusion of a competition the event promoter shall provide the SMMAF with documentation on results and, when applicable, injuries and suspension periods.

2. Event coordinator

2.1   An event coordinator shall be appointed for each competition.

2.2   During the course of the competition the event coordinator shall be the contact person for official authorities such as the police, the fire department and the governmental licensing authority.

2.3   The event coordinator shall manage all officials and personnel during the competition.

2.4   The event coordinator shall ensure that all officials and personnel perform their tasks as required.

3. Contestants

3.1   The contestant shall be at least 18 years of age.

3.2   The contestant shall be in good physical and mental health.

3.3   The contestant shall be well prepared to compete in mixed martial arts.

3.4 The contestant shall have documented experience of competing in full contact martial arts.

3.5 When entering a competition the contestant is responsible for ensuring that all relevant martial art experience is communicated to the matchmaker.

3.6 The contestant is limited to participating in one match per day.

4. Database

4.1 All information regarding a competition shall be stored in a database.

4.2 The contestants shall be registered in the database along with information about them, allowing the database to be used as a digital match book. It is the responsibility of the matchmaker to enter the contestants into the database.

4.3 Planned matches shall be entered into the database. This is the responsibility of the matchmaker.

4.4 Results from matches shall be entered into the database. This is the responsibility of the secretary.

4.5 When applicable, information on knockouts and suspensions shall be entered into the database as documented by the event physician. This is the responsibility of the event physician.

5. Matchmaking

5.1 A matchmaker with appropriate experience of mixed martial arts and matchmaking shall be responsible for matching contestants.

5.2 The matchmaker is charged with matching contestants based on all relevant facts regarding the contestants (weight, height, previous matches, other martial arts experience, previous knockouts and so forth). When possible, the matchmaker shall watch video footage of the contestants' previous matches.

5.3 All matches shall be evenly matched, taking the build and competitive experience of the contestants into account to ensure that only evenly matched contestants compete with each other. The previous experience of a contestant in other martial arts shall be taken into consideration.

5.4 The matchmaker shall ensure that all contestants as well as all planned matches are entered into the database.

6. Weight classes

6.1 Opposing contestants shall be closely matched in terms of weight. In heavyweight, however, a larger difference in weight is acceptable. The matchmaker shall determine a weight which both contestants of a planned match shall be able to reach on the day of the weigh-in. This weight shall be approved in good time by both contestants and event promoter.

6.2 In the event of a title match set weight classes apply.

6.3 Weight classes:
Flyweight: −56.7 kg (125 lbs)
Bantamweight: −61.2 kg (135 lbs)
Featherweight: −65.8 kg (145 lbs)
Lightweight: −70.3 kg (155 lbs)
Welterweight: −77.1 kg (170 lbs)
Middleweight: −83.9 kg (185 lbs)
Light Heavyweight: −93.0 kg (205 lbs)
Heavyweight: −120.2 kg (265 lbs)
Super Heavyweight: +120.2 kg (over 265 lbs)

7. Weigh-in

7.1 The contestant shall meet a set weight within a prescribed time at the official weigh-in for the competition, as supervised by officials appointed by the event promoter.

7.2 At the weigh-in the contestant shall produce photo identification and hand in a certificate for negative hepatitis B, hepatitis C and HIV tests. The tests must be no older than one year.

7.3 The contestant shall be weighed without clothes no later than

3 hours and no earlier than 32 hours before the match starts.

7.4   If the contestant weighs more than the set weight at the first weigh-in he/she is allowed to weigh in again later. Weight loss is however limited to 3% of the body weight on the first weigh-in. If the first weigh-in takes place one day before the match a weight-loss of 5% is allowed.

8. Event physician and Medical exam

8.1   One licensed physician shall be appointed event physician.

8.2   The event promoter shall hand over documentation on the contestants before the medical exam that takes place before the match. This documentation shall contain certificates for negative hepatitis B, hepatitis C and HIV tests.

8.3   The event physician shall examine all contestants before the match. If a contestant is deemed by the event physician to be out of shape, suffering from injury or illness, affected by drugs or narcotics, mentally unbalanced, or in any other way not fit to participate in the match, the contestant shall not be allowed to compete. Check-list: heart, blood pressure, pulse, lungs, hearing, teeth, evidence of a hernia, musculature, skin, negative hepatitis B, hepatitis C and HIV tests.

8.4   An event physician shall be present during each match. The event physician shall interrupt the match if he/she deems a contestant unfit to continue. In such an event the event physician shall immediately call for the attention of the referee by throwing a towel into the ring or sounding a signal.

8.5   If a contestant needs assistance in getting back to the corner for the round break, he/she shall be examined by the event physician, who among other things shall examine balance and reflexes when the contestant is standing without support.

8.6   After a match is concluded the event physician shall examine the contestants. When applicable, injuries and suspected injuries shall be documented.

8.7 The contest physician shall always consider a worst case-scenario. This means that he/she shall be risk averse when making judgement calls.

8.8 If the event physician finds it necessary for the contestant to have further examinations he/she shall send the contestant to the hospital.

8.9 In the event of a suspected injury (for example a light concussion), the event physician is allowed to detain the contestant for further observation. The contestant shall in such an event stay on site (or, if applicable, the competition hotel) so that the event physician can conduct a follow-up exam within a couple of hours. At such a follow-up exam the event physician shall determine whether the contestant needs to be sent to a hospital for further examination and care, or recommend follow-up treatment, or if the contestant is in no need of any further care. At the follow-up exam all such decisions and conclusions shall be documented and added to the overall documentation required to be handed in to the MMA Association by the event physician.

8.10 The event physician shall document, when applicable, knockouts and the exams that followed in hospitals or elsewhere, periods of suspension and the like.

9. Referee

9.1 Every match shall be overseen by a licensed referee.

9.2 The referee shall be dressed in a shirt and dress trousers, and shall wear soft shoes so that no damage or discomfort is inflicted on the contestants.

9.3 The referee shall be physically fit in order to stay alert, close to the contestants and able to intervene when necessary so that the contestants' safety is kept on as high a level as possible.

9.4 The referee shall ensure that both contestants are wearing appropriate protection.

9.5 The referee shall ensure that all parties involved in the match abide by the rules.

9.6 The referee shall put the contestants' safety first and immediately stop a match if and when it is apparent that one is so superior that the other stands the risk of being injured, if one of the contestants is in a questionable position of disadvantage, or if one of the contestants is not defending him/herself properly.

9.7 The referee has three commands during the match: 'FIGHT' tells the contestants that the match has started; initially, after a time-out or after a round break. 'STOP' tells the contestants to cease fighting and stay in the current position. 'BREAK' tells the contestants to cease fighting, separate and assume a neutral position.

9.8 The referee shall stop the match if and when a contestant uses unauthorised techniques or breaks the rules.

9.9 The referee shall ensure that unauthorised techniques are not used to the advantage of one contestant.

9.10 The referee shall disqualify a contestant if he/she or his/her coaches deliberately, severely, or repeatedly break the rules.

9.11 The referee shall stop the match if anything is thrown onto the fighting area. If a coach or event physician throws in a towel or equivalent the match is to be stopped.

9.12 In the event of an accident or foul the referee can issue a time-out in the match, allowing for one of the contestants to recuperate in up to five minutes.

9.13 In the event of a foul consisting of a blow or kick to the groin area (a so-called low blow) the referee shall, upon request from the injured contestant, issue a time-out in up to five minutes, allowing him/her to recuperate.

9.14 The referee shall stop the match at the sound of the signal that marks the end of a round.

9.15 The referee shall raise the arm of the winner when the results of the match have been made public by the speaker.

10. Judge

10.1   Every match shall be judged and the score is to be kept by three SMMAF licensed judges.

10.2   The judges shall sit separate from the audience as well as each other.

10.3   The judges shall remain neutral during the course of the match other than when identifying a break of the rules. In such a case the judges shall notify the referee during the round break.

10.4   The judges shall keep score and award points to the contestants for each round independent of one another. They shall also independently fill out the scorecard for each round.

10.5   The winner of a round is awarded 10 points while his/her contestant is awarded 9 points for dominance, 8 points for substantial dominance and 7 points for total dominance. If the round is very even then both contestants are awarded 10 points.

10.6   At the end of a match the judges shall summarise the points for all rounds.

10.7   The judges shall hand over the scorecard with the results of the match clearly marked.

10.8   The judges are not allowed to leave their place until the match is over and the results have been relayed.

10.9   A person who functions as a manager, whether a written agreement exists or not, is forbidden from acting as either referee or judge in a match where he/she represents one of the contestants.

11. Supervisor

11.1   For each MMA competition the SMMAF must appoint a supervisor.

11.2   The supervisor shall ensure that all functions and areas of responsibility are handled in an appropriate manner.

11.3 The supervisor shall be available to staff from the state licensing authority.

11.4 The supervisor shall take note of the result and type of result in each match.

11.5 The supervisor shall ensure that the results are entered into the database upon completion of the competition.

11.6 When applicable, the supervisor shall assist the event physician with entering knockouts and suspension periods into the database upon completion of the competition.

11.7 The supervisor shall document and report all possible deviations to the SMMAF.

12. Timekeeper

12.1 A timekeeper shall be appointed to ensure correct timing of rounds as well as round breaks and time-outs in the match.

12.2 The timekeeper signals the start of each round.

12.3 The timekeeper shall indicate when fifteen seconds remain of a round break.

12.4 When the referee signals a time-out it shall not count as part of the round. The clock may not be stopped by anything other than a time-out signalled by the referee.

12.5 The timekeeper is responsible for keeping the time from the point where the referee stops the match. The timekeeper shall notify the referee when the time-out reaches 4.5 minutes and 5 minutes respectively.

13. Speaker

13.1 A speaker shall be appointed with the task of keeping officials, personnel and audience informed of the competition over a public address system.

13.2 The speaker shall announce the names of the contestants, ring corner and weight before they enter the ring.

13.3 The speaker shall call on the coaches to leave the fighting area before the match starts as well as when the timekeeper indicates that 15 seconds remains of the round break.

13.4 The speaker shall announce the number of the round before each round starts.

13.5 The speaker shall announce the name and ring corner of the winner.

14. Coaches (Seconds)

14.1 The contestant shall have no fewer than one and no more than three coaches.

14.2 The coaches are only allowed to enter the fighting area in close proximity to his/her contestant's ring corner during round break.

14.3 During the round break no more than two coaches are allowed onto the fighting area. All equipment must be removed from the ring at the end of the round break and the coaches must also ensure that the fighting area is kept dry and clean to prevent slipping.

14.4 During the round break the coaches are required to inform the referee of any injuries or other impediments acquired by the contestants.

14.5 The coaches shall bring towels to the ring so that if they find their contestant unable to continue they may throw in the towel, thus forfeiting the match.

14.6 The coaches can give advice, assistance and encouragement in a contained manner during the course of the match.

14.7 The contestants can be told off, warned or disqualified for violations of the rules made by his/her coaches.

15. Fighting area

15.1 The fighting area shall be well enclosed so that the contestants are not at risk of falling out. It may be a standard boxing ring or a ring with a safety fence.

15.2   Boxing ring: Sizes can vary; the basic requirement is a shock-absorbing floor that is fenced with 3–4 padded ring ropes expanded between 4 poles (ring corners). These corners must be padded. Measures must also be taken to ensure that the contestants are not injured if falling out of the ring (for example by use of a shock-absorbing floor outside of the ring area).

15.3   Ring with a safety fence: The purpose of the walled ring is to avoid the risk of contestants falling out of the ring during the fight and suffering injury. Sizes may vary, but the basic requirements are a shock-absorbing floor that is fenced with a plastic covered net (wall) stretched between 8 poles. These poles as well as the lower and upper rim around the net are to be covered in padding.

16. Length of the match

16.1   A match shall contain three rounds.

16.2   Each round shall last five minutes.

16.3   The round break shall last 90 seconds.

17. Compulsory equipment

17.1   Approved competition gloves provided by the event promoter.

17.2   Approved competition shorts made in a durable material and designed in such a way that they cannot inflict injury on any of the contestants.

17.3   A protective groin cup.

17.4   A gumshield.

18. Gauze and tape

18.1   Hands and knuckles may be wrapped in gauze.

18.2   Tape may be used for fastening as well as strengthening the gauze. The tape may not, however, cover the knuckles.

18.3   The velcro fastening on the match gloves shall be taped so that they do not come undone and injure either of the contestants.

18.4   Taping and wrapping shall be checked before the velcro fastening on the glove is taped.

18.5   The official checking taping and wrapping of hands shall clearly indicate that such an inspection has been made, for instance by signing the tape on the outside of the glove.

19. Approved techniques

19.1   Strikes, kicks and knees against head, body and legs in stand-up position.

19.2   Strikes against head, body and legs when the opponent is in an active ground position.

19.3   Kicks and knees against body and legs when the opponent is in an active ground position.

19.4   Throws and takedowns.

19.5   Submission techniques (locks and chokes, etc.).

20. Unauthorised techniques

20.1   Strikes, kicks or knees against the spine or the back of the head.

20.2   Strikes against the larynx or gripping of the same.

20.3   Elbow attacks.

20.4   Throws where the opponent is intended to land solely on his/her head and/or neck (so-called spiking).

20.5   Locks on fingers and toes (so-called small joint manipulation).

20.6   Stomps against the opponent's feet.

20.7   Stomps against the opponent when in an active ground position.

20.8   Kicks and knees against the head when the opponent is in an active ground position.

20.9   Heel kicks against the kidneys.

20.10   Kicks and knees against the head of an opponent in a standing position when being in an active ground position.

21. Fouls

21.1 Attacking an opponent who is prostrate or otherwise defence-less.

21.2 Rubbing the body (other than the face) with Vaseline, liniment or the like.

21.3 Excessive use of Vaseline.

21.4 Head-butting, eye-poking, biting, scratching, pinching, hair-pulling, groin attacks and poking the mouth or cuts.

21.5 Throwing the opponent out of the fighting area.

21.6 Grabbing of the rope or the safety fence.

21.7 Grabbing the opponent's shorts or gloves.

21.8 Attacking the opponent before the match has commenced, during a time-out, during the round break or after the match is over.

21.9 Attacking an opponent who is being examined by a judge or contest physician.

21.10 Attacking the opponent's groin area.

21.11 Competing in an unsportsmanlike manner that causes injury to the opponent.

21.12 Strikes aimed specifically against the throat, including gripping the opponent's larynx.

21.13 Swearing or using abusive language.

21.14 Making abusive gestures.

21.15 Ignoring the instructions of the referee.

21.16 Displaying aggressive behaviour towards the referee or other officials.

21.17 Interference by coaches.

21.18 Dropping/spitting out the gumshield on purpose.

21.19 Inactivity and passivity.

21.20 Simulating being hit in the groin area.

21.21 Contestants are not allowed to wear any metal objects, nor any jewellery during a match.

22. Falling

22.1 If a contestant falls to the ground due to a takedown, throw, hit, surprise or loss of balance the match continues as long as the contestant can put up a proper defence and takes an active ground position.

23. Strike down

23.1 If a contestant is struck down and can't put up a proper defence and/or stays down the referee shall interrupt the match immediately (known as Referee Stops Contest or RSC).

24. Warning

24.1 In the event of a lesser accidental offence (using an unauthorised technique or committing a foul) the referee shall interrupt the match, examine the condition of the contestant and issue a warning.

24.2 The referee can issue a deduction in points in conjunction with the warning.

25. Disqualification

25.1 In the event of an intentional, serious or repeated offence the referee as well as the supervisor may disqualify the contestant.

26. Restart in the same position

26.1 After a warning has been issued and an examination has been conducted by the event physician or similar, the match shall be restarted in the same position as before it was interrupted.

27. Restart after inactivity

27.1 The referee can restart the match in a neutral position (standing) if the contestants are in a stalemate or aren't actively seeking to better their position or actively working to gain advantage.

28. Types of results

28.1 Submission – The contestant surrenders by tapping the opponent three times or by verbally informing the referee.

28.2 Towel – The contestant's coaches stop the match by throwing in the towel.

28.3 The referee stops the match (Referee Stops Contest, RSC). The referee is required to do so if he deems the match to be too uneven, if one of the contestants isn't putting up a proper defence, if one of the contestants has been hit hard (including but not limited to so-called Technical KnockOut/TKO and KnockOut/KO), or if the recuperation time or a medical examination of a contestant has lasted for more than five minutes.

28.4 Judges' decision – Three judges name the winner.

28.5 Disqualification – If a contestant is disqualified the opponent is awarded the win.

28.6 Walkover – If an announced contestant is ready on site in the fighting area and gets stood up by the opponent he/she is awarded the win.

29. Criteria for judging

29.1 The contestant awarded a win in each round is the one who controls and dominates the match and who is most effective in the areas of striking (blows and kicks), fighting in a standing position, clinch (wrestling in a standing position), throws/takedowns, position control, striking during ground fights and attempted submission. The techniques should be well carried out. Uncoordinated aggression is not to be rewarded.

29.2 Lying on top in a guard position (meaning ground fighting with the opponent's legs around the upper body) shall only be considered a dominant position if the contestant attempts to finish the match (through effective striking or attempted submissions) or to improve his/her position (such as passing the guard). A contestant who solely pins the opponent down without active attempts to win shall not be considered dominant.

29.3 If the contestants are equal in their offensive play then defensive techniques shall be considered, including blocking strikes and kicks, defence against takedowns, and turning a bottom position into a top position or a standing position.

29.4 If the contestants are evenly matched both offensively and defensively the contestant who was most active and had attempted to win the most should be awarded the win.

30. Draw

30.1 If the score at the end of the match is even the match is ruled a draw.

30.2 In the event of a title match the judges must rule on a winner (i.e. state a winner on the scorecard).

31. No contest and scorekeeping in the event of an unintended foul

31.1 A match can be judged no contest (i.e. nullified). This can be done during or after a match.

31.2 Reasons for no contest include disruption or abandonment as a result of outside interference, after which it no longer can be continued.

31.3 If a contestant accidentally gets injured as a result of an unauthorised technique (such as head-butting) and if the match consequently has to be stopped, then the match shall be judged 'no contest' provided that the injury in question occurs during round one or two.

31.4 If a contestant is unable to continue fighting due to an unintended foul after the conclusion of round two, the points shall be totalled and a winner announced.

31.5 If an injury caused by an unintended foul during round one or two is made worse by authorised techniques and this injury causes the match to be disrupted during round three, then the points awarded until the match was stopped shall be added up.

32. Protest

32.1   If a contestant or his/her coaches finds the result of a match to be incorrect then a note of protest can be handed in to the event coordinator within 48 hours of the conclusion of the match.

32.2   A protest must be submitted from the contestant's club (Swedish athletes) or from the contestant's club/team or manager (foreign athletes), not from the contestant personally.

32.3   The protest shall contain information stating which match it concerns, what the protest is in regards to, reasons for protesting, and how the contestant feels that the match should be judged, as well as complete contact information.

32.4   The results of a match shall only be changed if an obvious mistake has been uncovered, meaning one that had an effect on the outcome of the match and was made by the referee, judges or another official.

33. Knockout

33.1   A contestant who was knocked out as a result of a blow to the head, or whose match was stopped by the referee because of several tough blows to the head, shall immediately be examined by the event physician.

33.2   The event physician is required to make an assessment on whether or not the contestant needs further examination in a hospital and/or an x-ray of the brain.

33.3   The event physician shall document, when applicable, knock-outs and the examinations that follow in hospitals or elsewhere, and periods of medical suspension.

34. Suspension – Quarantine

34.1 A contestant who was knocked out as a result of a blow to the head, or whose match was stopped by the judge because of several tough blows to the head which made him/her defenceless and unable to continue, shall not be permitted to participate in a competition or sparring match during a set period as specified in paragraph 34.3

34.2 The event physician has the right to decide on a suspension even if a match was not stopped if he/she deems it necessary due to the contestant having received many tough blows to the head.

34.3 One knockout – No earlier than four weeks after the match. Two knockouts during a period of three months – Three months after the match.
Two knockouts during a period of twelve months – One year after the match.

35. Doping

35.1 A positive test for doping as according to WADA's (World Anti-Doping Agency) and/or the IOC's (International Olympic Committee) doping list leads to immediate disqualification.

35.2 The contest coordinator is required to facilitate and aid in the implementation of doping tests run on the contestants.

35.3 If a contestant refuses to participate in a doping test he/she is immediately disqualified.

Picture Credits

Section 1:

1. A Gustafsson
2. A Gustafsson
3. A Gustafsson
4. A Gustafsson
5. A Gustafsson
6. A Gustafsson
7. A Gustafsson
8. A Gustafsson
9. A Gustafsson
10. Jimmy Eriksson
11. A Gustafsson
12. A Gustafsson

Section 2:

1. Urban Andersson/IBL picture agency
2. Jeff Chiu/AP/TT
3. Igor Vidyashev/IBL picture agency
4. Meddi Kabirzadeh
5. A Gustafsson
6. Jimmy Eriksson
7. A Gustafsson
8. A Gustafsson
9. A Gustafsson
10. A Gustafsson
11. A Gustafsson
12. Jimmy Eriksson

Section 3:
1. Meddi Kabirzadeh
2. Meddi Kabirdzadeh
3. A Gustafsson
4. Meddi Kabirzadeh
5. A Gustafsson
6. Meddi Kabirzadeh
7. A Gustafsson
8. A Gustafsson
9. Bingo Rimér
10. Bingo Rimér